REMEMBERING TANIZAKI JUN'ICHIRŌ AND MATSUKO

MICHIGAN MONOGRAPH SERIES IN JAPANESE STUDIES

NUMBER 82

CENTER FOR JAPANESE STUDIES
UNIVERSITY OF MICHIGAN

Remembering Tanizaki Jun'ichirō and Matsuko

Diary entries, interview notes, and letters, 1954–1989

Anthony H. Chambers

Including entries from the diaries of
Edward G. Seidensticker, courtesy of the
University of Colorado at Boulder

University of Michigan Press
ANN ARBOR

Published in the United States of America by

The University of Michigan Press

Manufactured in the United States of America

♾ Printed on acid-free paper

2020   2019   2018   2017   4   3   2   1

A CIP catalog record for this book is available from the British Library.

ISBN 978-0-472-07365-8 (hardcover : alk. paper)

ISBN 978-0-472-05365-0 (paper : alk. paper)

ISBN 978-0-472-12322-3 (e-book)

■ CONTENTS ■

INTRODUCTION

The novelist, playwright, and essayist Tanizaki Jun'ichirō (谷崎潤
一郎, 1886–1965) was still living when I visited Japan for the first
time, in 1964, but I never met him. Five years later I chose Tanizaki
when Edward Seidensticker (1921–2007), my mentor at Stanford and
the University of Michigan, proposed him as one of three writers I
might consider as the subject of my dissertation. (The others were
Iwano Hōmei [岩野泡鳴, 1873–1920] and Mori Ōgai [森鷗外, 1862–
1922].) Tanizaki's fiction became the principal focus of my activities
as a scholar and translator.

Seidensticker had met Tanizaki in 1954, translated two of his
most successful novels—*Some Prefer Nettles* (『蓼喰ふ蟲』, 1928–
29, trans. 1955) and *The Makioka Sisters* (『細雪』, 1943–48, trans.
1957)—and introduced to Western readers the famous essay *In Praise
of Shadows* (『陰影禮讚』, 1933–34, partial trans. 1954, full trans.,
with Thomas J. Harper, 1977). In 1965 he attended Tanizaki's wake
and funeral. It was shortly after the funeral that I met Seidensticker,
my new graduate school adviser, for the first time.

At his urging, I wrote to Tanizaki's widow and muse, Tanizaki
Matsuko (谷崎松子, 1903–91), in 1970, to introduce myself and ask
for her help with my studies. Seidensticker had described her as the

most elegant woman he had ever met, which made her sound intimidating, but the lady I met was not only elegant but also spontaneous, warm, and unpretentious.

She met Tanizaki in 1927, when he was forty-one years old and she was twenty-four. Each was married at the time: Tanizaki to his first wife, Ishikawa Chiyo (石川千代, 1896–1982), whom he had married in 1915; and Matsuko to Nezu Seitarō (根津清太郎, 1900–1956), whom she had married in 1923. Chiyo bore Tanizaki's only child, Ayuko (鮎子, 1916–94). In 1930 Tanizaki divorced Chiyo, who promptly married the poet Satō Haruo (佐藤春夫, 1892–1964) in an arrangement to which they had all agreed but one that nonetheless scandalized the conservative Japanese society. In fact Satō had met Chiyo before Tanizaki did and stayed in touch with her throughout her marriage. In 1931 Tanizaki married Furukawa Tomiko (古川丁未子, 1907–69), whom he had initially hired as an assistant. They separated in December 1932, as a romantic relationship had blossomed between Tanizaki and Nezu Matsuko. Tanizaki divorced Tomiko in 1933 and began living with Matsuko early in 1934; she reverted to her maiden name, Morita (森田). Tanizaki and Matsuko were married in 1935. They had no children together, but Tanizaki adopted Matsuko's daughter, Emiko (恵美子, 1929–2013).

If we allow for some idealization on the author's part, the depiction of Miss Oyū in The Reed Cutter (『蘆刈』, 1932) describes Matsuko as follows.

> Though Miss Oyū had several sisters . . . , she received special treatment as her parents' favorite, and all her whims were indulged. One reason may have been that Miss Oyū was the most beautiful of the sisters, but . . . the sisters themselves seemed to think of her as someone special and to take it for granted that everyone else would think so too. Being "a person of character," . . . Miss Oyū didn't ask people to treat her this way, nor was she arrogant or pushy, but everyone was extremely kind

to her, waiting on her as if she were a princess and allowing her to do as she pleased, determined not to let her suffer the slightest anxiety. They sought to keep her untouched by the everyday troubles of the world, even if it meant sacrificing themselves for her sake. It was Miss Oyū's nature to make everyone who came near her feel this way, including her parents, sisters, and friends. . . . Miss Oyū was treated as though she were the Kosobe family treasure. She never did the smallest chore herself, and her sisters looked after her like chambermaids; nor was there anything unnatural about this . . .—Miss Oyū seemed to accept the attention with the greatest innocence. (p. 32)

In the course of countless interviews, dinners, excursions in Kyoto, and trips to the theater over a period of nearly twenty years, Mrs. Tanizaki and I developed a close friendship. She asked me to think of her as my Japanese grandmother. I often felt as though I were participating in a sequel to *The Makioka Sisters*—as well I might, since Mrs. Tanizaki was the inspiration for Makioka Sachiko, and her younger sister Watanabe Shigeko (渡辺重子, 1907–74) inspired Makioka Yukiko. The first time I visited Mrs. Tanizaki's home, Shōchikukyo (湘竹居), in Yugawara, I watched the sisters act out what could have been a scene in the novel. When I praised the view of the garden from the living room, Mrs. Watanabe began, "It would be even better if . . ." Her voice trailed off, just as Yukiko's does in the book. "If the *hagi* were in bloom!" Mrs. Tanizaki said brightly, finishing her sister's sentence. They spoke with the unselfconscious courtesy of their generation.

I would telephone Mrs. Tanizaki when I arrived in Tokyo on my annual trips; she would announce that she had found a new restaurant for us to try. "Delicious!" she would exclaim (おおいしゅうございますの！). One evening, several of us set out in a hired car to sample her latest discovery. When the car pulled up in front of the restaurant, she cried, "Oh, this is the wrong place. But let's give it a try!" and sent her companion inside to ask for a table.

In the early years of our friendship, Mrs. Tanizaki would say that she could sense her late husband's spirit, as if it were hovering above our table, watching approvingly as we dined and chatted about his work. Over the years, however, a trend became evident in her reflections, as she came to focus less on memories of Jun'ichirō and more on her own life and thoughts. For my part, I came to consider her at least as interesting a person as her famous husband must have been.

In the late 1970s, I planned to collaborate on a biography of Tanizaki with the scholar and translator Paul McCarthy (with whom I have collaborated on two collections of short stories). Always eager to help, Mrs. Tanizaki introduced us to a number of people who had known her husband well. The biography never materialized, but I still have diary entries and notes from interviews with these memorable people.

> Howard S. Hibbett (b. 1920), translator of *Seven Japanese Tales, The Key, Diary of a Mad Old Man,* and *Quicksand.*
> Higuchi Tomimaro (樋口富麻呂, 1898–1981), artist, a friend of the Tanizakis
> Ichida Yae (市田ヤヱ, 1910–?), a friend of the Tanizakis
> Kataoka Nizaemon XIII (十三代目片岡仁左衛門, 1903–94), Kabuki actor
> Donald Keene (b. 1922), scholar of Japanese literature
> Okuyama Hatsuko (奥山初子, 1910–?), Tanizaki's favorite geisha
> Onoe Rokujirō (尾上六次郎, 1904–?), Tanizaki's guide in Yoshino
> Shigeyama Sensaku III (三世茂山千作, 1896–1986), Kyōgen master, a friend of the Tanizakis
> Harold Strauss (d. 1975), Tanizaki's editor at his English-language publisher, Alfred A. Knopf
> Takeda Ayuko (竹田鮎子, 1916–94), Tanizaki's daughter

Tanizaki Akio (谷崎昭夫, b. 1944), a son of Jun'ichirō's brother
  Seiji (谷崎精二)
Tanizaki Shūhei (谷崎終平, 1908–90), Tanizaki's youngest
  brother
Watanabe Shigeko (渡辺重子, 1907–74), one of Mrs. Tanizaki's
  younger sisters
Yamaguchi Kōichi (山口廣一, 1902–79), drama critic and
  director
Yamaguchi Mitsuko (山口光子, dates unknown), Tanizaki's
  next-door neighbor in Sumiyoshi in the early 1940s

The present book begins with several vivid passages from the diaries of Edward Seidensticker and a few excerpts from my own jour-
nals. Following these is a record of comments from Tanizaki Matsuko
and the others, both unsolicited and in response to questions; more
entries from my diaries; and excerpts from a few letters. I have included, in parentheses, the original Japanese wording of comments
when I made a note of it at the time. Inevitably, the observations are
subject to memory lapses (my sources' and my own) and partiality,
particularly on the part of Mrs. Tanizaki as the principal guardian of
her husband's legacy. Contradictions among the accounts of various
witnesses, too, reflect subjectivities and varying perspectives. If the
overall impression is one of hagiography, this is due in part to the
affection and gratitude I felt toward Mrs. Tanizaki, and in part to the
fact that almost everyone I met was well disposed toward Matsuko
and Jun'ichirō. The principal exception was Tanizaki's nephew Akio
(昭男), who urged me to read a short screed by Jun'ichirō titled
"On the Occasion of the Fall of Singapore" (「シンガポールの陥
落に際して」, March 1942) because, he said, it demonstrates his
uncle's support for Japanese aggression in World War II. Akio also
told me that he preferred the writings of Satō Haruo over those of
Jun'ichirō. I failed to take notes during my dinner with Akio and his

son Kan (閑, a student of mine), and I confess that I didn't seek out other negative perspectives.

The dual focus throughout this collection is on Tanizaki Jun'ichirō and Tanizaki Matsuko. Some of the information presented here is available in Japanese publications. Very little of it has been published in Western sources, and much appears here for the first time in any language. The accounts will be of particular interest to specialists in modern Japanese literature and fans of Tanizaki's novels. They will also, I believe, give readers a sense of the personalities of these two remarkable people.

Several good English-language overviews and studies of Tanizaki's career and works have been published, complementing the many translations of his writings into English, Italian, French, and other languages. About Tanizaki Matsuko, almost nothing is available in Western languages. In Japanese we have her three memoirs, her collected poetry, and studies and memoirs by many others. See "References" in this volume.

In most entries I refer to Tanizaki Matsuko as "Mrs. Tanizaki." If I were writing in Japanese, I would probably refer to her as "Matsuko fujin" (松子夫人), which is perhaps more polite but would convey little to most readers of English. I always addressed her in person as "Okusama" (奥様), an honorific for a married woman.

■ ACKNOWLEDGMENTS ■

Paul McCarthy accompanied me on several occasions, Robert Campbell (a student at the time, now Director-General, National Institute of Japanese Literature) on some others. I'm indebted to them for their insights and for asking important questions that I hadn't thought of.

Professor Laurel Rasplica Rodd, of the University of Colorado at Boulder, and David M. Hays, of the university's archives, generously made it possible for me to read and transcribe parts of Edward Seidensticker's diaries in the University Libraries.

Everyone I interviewed received me with great kindness and generosity. For further insights, introductions, and kindnesses, I'm also indebted to Professor Chiba Shunji, of Waseda University; the late Ibuki Kazuko, Tanizaki's former research assistant and amanuensis; and Watanabe Chimako, Matsuko's daughter-in-law and the inspiration for several of Tanizaki's characters. Mr. Hara Koichi, of Doshisha University, assisted with interviews I conducted in 1977. My research over the years has been supported by a Fulbright scholarship and grants from the American Philosophical Society, the Japan Foundation, the Japan-United States Friendship Commission, the Associated Kyoto Program, and Wesleyan University. Finally, I'm deeply grateful to the staff of the University of Michigan Press and the comments of its anonymous reviewers.

DIARY ENTRIES AND LETTERS

EDWARD SEIDENSTICKER ON HIS FIRST MEETING WITH
TANIZAKI JUN'ICHIRŌ AND MATSUKO, 1954

I met Tanizaki last Sunday, a pleasant old man, very straightforward for a Japanese. He had little to say about his writing, which
one would gather bores him, though he did concede that Tade Kuu
Mushi [*Some Prefer Nettles*] should do as well in English as anything
of his. His wife, the Sachiko of Sasame Yuki [*The Makioka Sisters*],
was there too, graceful and poised in a purple kimono—quite without the simpering way so many Japanese ladies of good family—or
who would like to appear of good family—have. (Seidensticker's diary, 4/2/1954, Edward Seidensticker Papers, 1–2, Archives, University
of Colorado Boulder Libraries)

SEIDENSTICKER ON TANIZAKI'S DEATH,
AND HIS CONDOLENCE CALL, 1965

Tanizaki-sensei died early on the morning of this sweltering day
[7/30/65]. I was to learn sometime in the next few days and all the

reports were that he had been doing very well since his operation. All of a sudden he stopped eating and his kidneys stopped functioning. His life was less by about half of one percent than Kafū's—just over 949 months, to just under 954 for Kafū. I wonder if he did not have a presentiment that such might be the case. He always seemed so aware of the exact difference in their ages, as though that were precisely the margin allowed him.

Mrs. Shimanaka called at about nine, and my immediate impulse was to wipe away some of the sweat with which I had been drenched the whole night through and take the first train for Yugawara. She suggested that I go in a Chūō Kōron car, and I promptly accepted, not suspecting what later, to my considerable consternation, seemed to be the case, that the car was dispatched for my private use. [Chūō Kōron (C.K., CK) is Tanizaki's principal publisher. Shimanaka Hōji was the president of the company.] Only one young Chūō Kōron functionary, the man who arranged things so nicely for our visit to Tanizaki last year, was with me.

The trip seemed an eternity. The air, even inside an air-conditioned car, quite unbreathable until past Fujisawa, the traffic lawless and impenetrable. A demonstration of how useless the new freeways are, essentially—you descend at Haneda, and to on to Yokohama, have to make your way through endless jammed alleys to the national highway.

The beach at Yugawara bright and noisy with the summer, and up on the hill, a hush. Miss Ibuki, in tears, took me in to see the corpse, laid out on a bed in a room scarcely big enough for anything more (the bedrooms on both sides of a steamy hall, extraordinarily small for a house into which so much money has obviously gone), watched over by the son-in-law, Kanze Hideo. The color of the face was rather horrible—suggesting that there had indeed been a failure of the kidneys—but it had a half-smile on it, and a childish quality that in other circumstances might have been called charming. And that was that—the last glimpse of probably the most important man I shall ever know.

I waited in the living room for an hour or so hoping to be able to speak to Mrs. Tanizaki. Miss Ibuki and Takizawa from C.K. came over to talk from time to time, as did a number of reporters, but Shimanaka seemed very stand-offish, to make me wonder whether I had done the wrong thing, whether I might seem to be trying to get my name in the papers. And another thing bothered me: there were reporters all over the place and swarms of CK people making complicated plans, but there were no writers except for the brother, Tanizaki Seiji. I had, I feared, indeed been forward—but certainly with Mrs. Shimanaka's encouragement.

At length Mrs. Tanizaki did receive me. She looked very tiny, as if shrunken by the shock, and was very sweet—told me I must look after my leg, as if it were the most important living or once-living thing in the vicinity. I was almost in tears. A glimpse of Mrs. Watanabe, also tiny, and Emiko, who seems to have reacted in the direction of inflation, not the pretty little thing she used to be.

I was sent off to Tokyo in a taxi, lest I do damage to my leg—this at Chūō Kōron expense, though I shall insist upon re-paying. The tariff I set down for the record, since I shall probably never again have such a long taxi ride: ¥5,540. Very cheap, I say—less than a day of Mr. Hertz. All the way back I wondered whether I had done the right thing or not—and of course I could reach no conclusion, save that my motives were good, and Mrs. Shimanaka, whatever Mr. S. may have thought, did encourage me. The attached clippings, from the Nikkei and the Asahi, make me feel that I did, after all, the right thing. My name in the papers is about the last thing I expected, but I am sure that had my behavior been in bad taste, the naughty Asahi would have rewarded it with silence.

I affix a second article, again from the Asahi, in which I am mentioned. The note I think to be one of approval, but I am not as worried about the problem as I was yesterday. The reporter is clearly trying to suggest that there were more condolence calls than there actually were, and so I suppose the ones that did occur were all to the good. (Seidensticker's diary, 7/30/1965, Edward Seidensticker Papers, 3–6, Archives, University of Colorado Boulder Libraries)

SEIDENSTICKER ON TANIZAKI'S WAKE, 1965

In the evening it took me about forty-five minutes to get down to the Kioi-chō Fukudaya. . . . Presently Howard Hibbett came around, and we departed for the Tanizaki wake in a most grand manner: seen from the Kioi-chō Fukudaya to the Toranomon Fukudaya in the Kioi-chō Fukudaya's car.

The wake was rather splendid, although I felt very silly hobbling about for the movie cameras. Worse than silly—if I seemed like a ham to myself, what must I have seemed like to others. And there was the awful business of kneeling down and leaving to get back up again, and the impossibility of greeting anyone properly.

But as I have said, it was all very grand. Japanese funeral customs must be among the most civilized in the world, solemn without a touch of the maudlin, lively but not in the least noisy. The only thing I disliked was the picture of the sensei [i.e., of Tanizaki]. It was in color, and had a yellowish tinge that reminded me of the corpse. After the incense thing I was shown to a room swarming with geniuses: Kawabata [Yasunari], that Sōgi no Meijin; Funabashi [Seiichi], Mishima [Yukio], the president of Kadokawa; and she-writers too, Enji Fumiko and Koyama Itoko. The list could go on and on—Itō Sei, Ooka Shōhei. I think it a fine thing that a wake should give you a sense of being in the very middle of life. And the talk was in no sense funereal—numbers of not at all flattering remarks about the sensei's work. Mishima gave us a long account of the dirty life in Havana before the revolution. Very dirty indeed.

Afterwards Howard and I made our way to the Ginza, to drink for couple of hours in a place with the odd name Oshijō, which seems to mean something like "the castle that withstood the siege." (Seidensticker's diary, 8/2/1965, Edward Seidensticker Papers, 3–6, Archives, University of Colorado Boulder Libraries)

SEIDENSTICKER ON TANIZAKI'S FUNERAL, 1965

Down to the New Japan [Hotel] at noon (it is falling to pieces at a great rate, and is coming to look like the Dai Ichi minus the crowds) to meet Donald Keene. We were to have lunch together, but Miss Ibuki [Kazuko] had called earlier to say that there was not time; and so, after a beer, we sped off to the Tanizaki funeral, at the Aoyama Cemetery. K. looked perfectly awful—wild-haired and drawn. He had a long story of a bad night with Yoshida Kenichi but it did not sound bad enough to explain his appearance. I suspect nervous exhaustion. He kept snapping at people, rather as I must have done in the worst times before I picked up and left this dear country.

The funeral itself was quiet and tasteful, though there was one bad moment for which the organizers can scarcely be held responsible. Takamine Hideko put on a real act, loud, strangled weeping and all that when she offered up her flowers. If I felt like the principal ham yesterday evening, I certainly had every right to feel outdone today. Kyō Machiko, who I am sure was the more grief-stricken of the two, was quiet and composed. There was none of that awful business, the worst thing about Japanese funerals, of going over the details of the last illness.

And not, for poor Matsuko, the sudden access of neglect—the quick withdrawal of the <u>bundan</u> [literary community]. Of course he had little commerce with it and so, perhaps, the change will be less for her than for most—much less than for Mrs. Nakaya [Ukichirō?], for example.

Keene said that he did a rather horrible thing with his condolence telegram—addressed it to Tanizaki Sachiko. Well, as Howard Hibbett, also at the funeral, pointed out, it could have been worse: he might have called her Satsuko [the apparently sadistic daughter-in-law in Tanizaki's *Diary of a Mad Old Man*]. (Seidensticker's diary, 8/3/1965, Edward Seidensticker Papers, 3–6, Archives, University of Colorado Boulder Libraries)

I meant to record that at the end of the Tanizaki visit on Tuesday I was shown into the Sensei's study, looking down over bamboo and loquats and the sea, and allowed to sit in the chair from which he dictated his last works, and I felt as if even the least effective of mediums could bring us together. On his book shelves the presence of a single modern novelist was to be detected: Kōda Rohan. But Takizawa tells me that the Sensei spoke of only one man as "Sensei," and that was Natsume Sōseki. (Seidensticker's diary, 8/20/1965, Edward Seidensticker Papers, 3–6, Archives, University of Colorado Boulder Libraries)

MY (CHAMBERS'S) FIRST MEETING
WITH TANIZAKI MATSUKO, 1971

Wednesday morning I finally got up my courage and called Mrs. Tanizaki. She has a thin voice, but a pleasant one, is, as one would expect very polite and self-effacing, though not untalkative, I should think. And of course there's the Osaka accent, more than a bit hard to catch on the phone. She invited us to dinner at her daughter's house in Akasaka Saturday night. (My diary, 2/24/71)

We found the house in Akasaka without much trouble--, 観世栄夫 [Kanze Hideo], her son-in-law's house. Mrs. Tanizaki is a small, graceful woman, slender, with a thin face, fine skin and hair, and doesn't look more than fifty, though she's nearly seventy [she was sixty-seven in fact]. Her gestures and bearing, the way she stands and walks just slightly bent at the knees, reminded me of an Utamaro print. She speaks very clearly, readily repeats and rephrases for us when we don't understand, and her Osaka accent was no problem for us. She said, in fact, that she uses something close to standard Japanese when she's in Tokyo because she is embarrassed by the stares and oblique looks she gets when she uses Osaka Japanese in public. Tanizaki liked the Osaka dialect and would say to her, 「大阪弁を話せばいいのに」 (You should speak Osaka-ben).

She is, by reputation, the epitome of the old-school, high-class Japanese lady. She's extremely graceful, polite, and considerate, but not exactly dainty, far from delicate, and not particularly diffident or self-effacing. She says what she thinks in an unexpectedly lively way, sometimes with sweeping gestures of her arms over her head and bursts of laughter (covered with a handkerchief). I asked what her favorites were among Tanizaki's works--she replied Shōshō Shigemoto no haha [*Captain Shigemoto's Mother*, 1949] and In'ei raisan [*In Praise of Shadows*, 1933]. [She later included *The Makioka Sisters* among her favorites (4/19/71).] When I told her that <u>Shigemoto</u> was also [my wife] Susan's favorite, she stretched out her hand and said "hakushu!" ["Shake!"]. She's a strong woman, poised, confident, relaxed, and enjoys people; she's extremely well read, sharp, observant, and talkative.

From the Kanze house we went to a restaurant in Roppongi [actually, Toranomon] called 福田家 [Fukudaya], run by old friends of the Tanizakis and frequented by Tanizaki himself. The committee that determines winners of the Tanizaki-shō [literature prize] meets there—Niwa Fumio [丹羽文雄, 1904–2005], Funahashi [Seiichi 舟橋聖一, 1904–76], Mishima [Yukio], Takeda Taijun [武田泰淳, 1912–76], and was it Enchi Fumiko [円地文子, 1905–86]? An elegant place, lovely garden, big, pure Japanese rooms. The room we ate in had a big Tanizaki kakemono [hanging-scroll] in the tokonoma [alcove] with the characters 聴歆 [*ichō*, "prick up your ears and listen", signed 潤一郎 書].

Mrs. Tanizaki took to Susie right away. She was especially impressed when Susie casually picked out an oddly shaped bowl to admire, and the serving lady said it was made by the famous Kitaoji Rosanjin [北大路 魯山人, 1883–1959]. お眼が高い ["You have a good eye"], Mrs. Tanizaki said.

Almost immediately after we got settled at Fukuda's, she launched in on how Japan has changed, how young people nowadays are depraved and don't recognize the beauty of old Japan. It's no wonder Mishima died, she said. She was most enthusiastic and animated about Mishima. She praised his gentleness, politeness and consideration, and exclaimed over and over about his mujaki na warai [artless laugh]--she'd never seen anything like it. She met him at the Tanizaki-shō meeting a week before his death [25 November 1970]: he laughed as usual and showed no sign of what was on his mind—kurai tokoro wa nakatta ["There was nothing gloomy about him"]. He was strong--takumashii—and so much stronger than Akutagawa Ryūnosuke. Mishima never had to look up things as he wrote, she said, and he never crossed out or made other changes as he wrote.

Akutagawa she met in 1925 or 6 [actually, 1927], shortly before his death. He was absolutely brilliant, and his eyes were wonderful, beautiful, like nothing she'd seen before—sumikitta me [perfectly clear eyes]. But he was yowayowashii [delicate], especially compared to Mishima; otonashii [gentle and quiet] but shinkeishitsu [high-strung]; and she sensed then that he looked like someone who would die soon. Tanizaki himself said the same in retrospect. "Shinisō na hito deshita" [He looked like a man who was about to die].

Another celebrity she talked of was Jean Paul Sartre, who came to Japan several years ago and said what he regretted most was that he couldn't meet Tanizaki Jun'ichirō. But he did meet Mrs. Tanizaki, at Hōnen'in [site of the Tanizaki graves]. He had read everything of Tanizaki's that he could get his hands on, loved it, and discerned the 母 ["mother"] theme running through everything.

But she loved best to talk about her husband, especially to reminisce about him with the ladies of the Fukudaya.

Tanizaki was interested in *people* more than anything else [she said], more than nature, which, she agreed, doesn't play a particularly important role in his writings.

He lived as thoroughly Western a life as he could in Yokohama [1921-23], [she continued,] eating nothing but Western food and even wearing his shoes in the house. But his interests didn't abruptly change in 1923 [after the great earthquake and his move to Western Japan]; he was interested in old Japanese literature from the beginning. He didn't premeditate the move to Kansai, [but] rather fled there after the earthquake [out of necessity] and gradually settled down.

He was stubborn (一本気) and gruff, yelled at the servants, and brushed Matsuko away gruffly (urusai!) ["don't be a nuisance!"] when she tried to straighten his lapels for a picture. When he was old and failing, he stopped doing it and stopped yelling at the maids; and frightening as it had been to be yelled at, they missed it when he stopped.

He had very strong likes and dislikes and never hesitated to express them. She used the word *hageshii* [harsh]. For one thing, he disliked the Edokko [son-of-Edo] side of Izumi Kyōka—Kanazawa kara kita no ni ["And he's from Kanazawa!"].

Tanizaki kept a list of names he'd like to use sometime; Otokuni was one of them, and it has no particular significance in Yume no ukihashi ["The Bridge of Dreams," 1959). Tadasu, of course, does [have particular significance]—it's the same as in Tadasu no mori

[Tadasu Woods, at Shimogamo, in Kyoto]. Tanizaki liked his house at Shimogamo the best [of all his residences], and that described in Ukihashi is exactly the same [as his own].

Mrs. Tanizaki likes 武州公秘話 [*The Secret History of the Lord of Musashi*, 1935] a lot. Tanizaki made notes for a sequel, including a story outline and characters, but never finished writing it. She is now editing his notes, plans to publish them.

She urged me to translate Bushūkō [*The Secret History*], also mentioned 途上 ["On the Road," 1924), 人面疽 ["The Growth With a Human Face," 1918], 富美子の足 ["Fumiko's Feet," 1919], and 金色の死 ["A Golden Death," 1914], which Mishima discusses in his 作家論 [Essays on Writers] and apologized profusely to Mrs. Tanizaki for discussing when he knew that Tanizaki hadn't liked it.

We returned to the Kanze house around 10:30 after a delicious dinner. Mrs. Tanizaki urged me to borrow several volumes of the [new] 全集 [*Complete Works*] to read things not included in the old one; she also gave me an autographed copy of her book *Ishōan no yume* (which she calls a key to his works). (My diary, 2/27/71)

MY BUSY DAY IN KYOTO WITH MRS. TANIZAKI
AND HER SISTER, 1971

Susie and I met at Kyoto Station in the morning. [Nagaeda] Shun'ichi was with us too, having arrived by night train from Tokyo. [Susan and Shun'ichi's mother worked with Living National Treasure artist Serizawa Keisuke, who designed at least one of Tanizaki's books.] We called Mrs. Tanizaki at her sister's house—her sister being Watanabe Shigeko, or Yukiko of *The Makioka Sisters*. She said by all means to bring Shun'ichi along, too.

We took a cab to Hōnen'in, Mrs. Tanizaki having told us that the Watanabe house is right across from the temple's back gate. The house is in fact perched on a hillside across the street from and below the temple, set back all alone from the street, the only house in sight. The house faces west, with big sliding doors on the south, too, looking out on a pair of beautiful shidarezakura [weeping cherry trees]. But the real view is to the west, out over the northeastern part of Kyoto. A broad veranda over the hillside commands a wide, lovely view, and a brook flows just below the house. The most conspicuous feature inside the house is that it is full of cats—mostly strays rescued by Mrs. Watanabe, according to Mrs. Tanizaki. [The house, designed by Mrs. Watanabe's late husband, is no longer standing.]

Mrs. Watanabe is delightful. Small, but not so thin as one would expect from reading The [Makioka] Sisters. Her face in fact almost gives the impression of being round. Her hair is silvery, and she wears heavy facial make-up—heavier than Matsuko. Oddly, she has almost no chin. Her voice is faint and not often heard, unless she speaks directly to you. She is not timorous or even terribly shy, I suppose; she chatted pleasantly with both Susie and Shun'ichi. But she is quiet and unobtrusive, particularly in contrast to her sister. The point is made several times in The Sisters too—Sachiko [corresponding to Tanizaki Matsuko] is asked to look old, or even to stay home, for Yukiko's [who corresponds to Shigeko] miai [meetings with prospective husbands], because she [unintentionally] draws all the attention herself. It's too true.

From the house we walked up to Hōnen'in. Strolling through the garden, we arrived at the office of the temple. All the doors were closed, and no one was in sight; but a block of wood and a wooden mallet were suspended from the eaves, with instructions to strike three times. Mrs. Tanizaki positioned herself in front of the door, and nodded to Shigeko, who took up the mallet and gave the block three resounding knocks, whereupon a handsome, diffident, young monk on his knees slid open the door. "Tanizaki de gozaimasu" ["My name is Tanizaki"], said Mrs. Tanizaki, in her elegantly hesitant way, dignified but not haughty or affected. The young monk was a model of diffidence and courtesy, charmingly boyish and attentive. He told us that the abbot was in bed with a cold. Mrs. Tanizaki said that was too bad, and gave the young priest several presents to deliver to the abbot. (Mrs. Watanabe had been carrying them, and slipped them to Mrs. Tanizaki at the right moment.) Then we strolled into the inner part of the temple. In a small, inner courtyard stand several huge "chiritsubaki" ["scattering camellias"], noted for the fact that their petals fall one by one, on most camellias the entire flower falls at once--like a decapitated head, which explains why many Japanese don't like camellias. We were then shown into the main hall. In front of the altar is a raised platform of highly polished dark wood. On this platform, 25 chrysanthemum blossoms are arranged in a pyramid pointing toward the altar, away from the viewer. The high polish of the wood reflects the flowers like the surface of a pond. (The 25 represent the 25 bodhisattvas, we are told.) It is in this hall that Tanizaki's 7th anniversary ceremony will be held.

The young priest then told us that the abbot would get up to see Mrs. Tanizaki, so wouldn't we wait and have some tea. We were ushered to a reception room—a small room packed with easy chairs and serving as the entrance to a formidable vault. Tea—the tea-ceremony type in beautiful bowls--was brought with delicious little cakes to be savored while we waited. Shortly the abbot came in. A cheerful, likable man of 60 or more, short and stocky with a very pleasant face and manner. The reason he appeared at all, and the reason Mrs. Tanizaki had gone [to the temple], was to make arrangements for Tanizaki's 7th [death] anniversary ceremony. He died on July 30 [1965]; the ceremony could be held on May 30 or June 30--auspicious ceremonies can be held late [she explained], but not early; sad ones are often held early, hence the preference for May or June when the heat wouldn't be so oppressive. June 30 was finally decided upon after some discussion. With this decision made, we left. As we reached the door, the abbot sent the young priest back to fetch the furoshiki [cloths] that Mrs. Tanizaki's gifts had been wrapped in. Mrs. Tanizaki protested, but the furoshiki were duly brought and returned.

On the way out of the temple offices, we decided to go up to visit Tanizaki's grave. "I'm fine going downhill," she said as she inched her way up the steps, "but I do have trouble on the way up." This was virtually the only sign of age we've noticed in her. At the grave she knelt for a few minutes while the three of us stood nearby. I asked her whose stone is beside Tanizaki's. It is that of Mr. Watanabe, Shigeko's husband, the "Mimaki" of *The Makioka Sisters*. Eventually they [she and Mrs. Watanabe] will all be buried there, I gather.

Mrs. Tanizaki had hired a taxi and driver for the day, a Mr. Nakajima [Yoshizō (中島吉三)], whom Mrs. Watanabe often uses. A pleasant and very talkative Kyoto man of 40 or 50, extremely well versed in Kyoto history and sights. As he drove he poured out a steady stream of information about Kyoto place-names, ancient sites, and miscellaneous lore of every kind. He drove us first toward Nanzenji; just north of Nanzenji is a short street lined with spacious villas and extraordinary restaurants, and cherry trees! We alighted to take pictures.

Not far from this street is the house that Tanizaki and Matsuko lived in first in Kyoto [in fact, right after WWII], on the bank of a tiny stream called 白川 [Shirakawa]: 左京区南禅寺下河原町 52). [The house is no longer standing.]

Nakajima-san then drove us west, beyond the Golden Pavilion to Haradani 原谷, a hill covered with weeping cherries. We strolled through virtual arcades of blossoms, caverns, and tunnels, feeling as though we were acting out part of *The Makioka Sisters*, savoring the blossoms and taking pictures of one another.

By coincidence, Mrs. Tanizaki took us to lunch at a restaurant I'd been to before, near Ginkakuji [the Silver Pavilion]—白水園

[Hakusuien], famous for miso-tofu. After lunch we strolled down the street to Hakusasonsō 白沙村荘, the garden of [the late artist] Hashimoto Kansetsu [橋本関雪, 1883–1945,the grandfather of Mrs. Tanizaki's daughter-in-law, Watanabe Chimako 渡辺千萬子]. The garden is rather spacious, full of stone lanterns, grotesque and curious trees, and stone Buddhist images [羅漢] with a wild assortment of faces—laughing, suspicious, angry, sleepy.

Then we sped off to Gion to see the Miyako Odori [Dance, 京踊り]. After sipping tea and [nibbling] cakes prepared in full view by two lavishly dressed *maiko [female dancers]*, we took our seats, precisely in the center of the front section, with our legs stretched comfortably into an aisle. Mrs. Watanabe was with us again, and it was fun to watch the two sisters chattering and twittering together like little girls. The choreographer, an old friend of the Tanizakis, and about whom Tanizaki wrote, is Inoue Yachiyo (井上八千代), a Living National Treasure [1905–2004]. We met her on the way to our seats—a tiny, elderly lady with round, wire-rimmed glasses. Again there was the slipping of gifts from Mrs. Watanabe to Mrs. Tanizaki [and on to Inoue-sensei]. The crowds were heavy on the way out, and so we were all slipped through a business room, on a sort of VIP route, as a shortcut to the street. Mrs. Tanizaki apologized to us for not getting better seats, though they were clearly the best seats in the house.

Finally, Mrs. Tanizaki took Shun'ichi and me to a Gion restaurant--鳥居本 [Toriimoto]: odd food, apparently derived ultimately from Chinese food and gradually evolved as it worked its way to Kyoto and Gion. We had a small room to ourselves, slightly elevated, with gardens on two sides and the sound of running water. Dinner was served on o-zen—small, individual tables. The dishes were all in a drawer of the o-zen—we were asked to take them out, and the food was placed on them, course by course. [* indicates favorites of Tanizaki's.]

1. sake: *taruzake*, with a delicate fragrance of wood
2. soup: *kenchin-jiru*, a thin soup with a delicate flavor and tiny pieces of chicken, gobō [burdock], carrot, and peas.
3. 2 pieces of sushi wrapped in sasa [bamboo-grass] leaves, like mochi [rice cakes].
4. sashimi buried in *nattō**
5. sweet *umeboshi* [pickled plum] tempura
6. two *ayu no shioyaki* [trout, grilled with salt], with two small green peppers
7. chicken and carrots, cooked in a pressure cooker
8. *karashidōfu* ["pepper tofu"]—slightly tangy
9. soup containing rice, fish (*amadai*, also known as *buji*, a kind of bream), and a cherry leaf*
10. very thin, cleansing soup—*hashi-arai* ["chopstick-wash"], with a cherry blossom in it
11. Rice and tsukemono [pickles]; tea.

Mrs. Tanizaki apologized that she wouldn't be able to show us around the next day. She had to rush back to Tokyo on the 20th to see Mrs. Mishima, who has been busy and hard to reach because of the *"Tate no Kai"* [Shield Society] trial going on now. (My diary, 5/13/71, describing events of April 19)

MY ACCOUNT OF THE OBSERVANCE OF THE SEVENTH
ANNIVERSARY OF TANIZAKI'S DEATH, 1971

An invitation to the seventh anniversary ceremony came several days ago from Mrs. Tanizaki. It's to be held at Hōnen'in on June 30, at 11:00 a.m. The invitation is beautifully written, but in fact seems to have been printed by some subtle process that reproduces her own handwriting in sumi [Japanese ink] on rice paper. Only my name was actually written [by hand], and not by Mrs. Tanizaki, I believe, comparing the script. The envelope clearly was addressed by someone else. The reply card was addressed to Mrs. Tanizaki, care of 渡辺清治 [Watanabe Seiji, her son, who was adopted by her sister]. The address is 京都左京区鹿ヶ谷法然院町). (My diary, 6/21/71)

Susie and I met at Hōnen'in at 10:30. Today was not precisely the anniversary, since Tanizaki died July 30, 1965. The years are counted as Japanese ages used to be. [Only six twelve-month periods had elapsed, but if we count the year 1965, 1971 was the seventh year in which he has been deceased.] As for the month: joyous celebrations, such as one's 80th birthday, may be postponed but never held in advance, while ceremonies marking sad occasions may be held early, but not late. Mrs. Tanizaki, mindful of the Kyoto heat of July, scheduled the ceremony one month early, despite fears of rain. The day turned out to be pleasantly cool for this time of year, and slightly overcast with no trace of rain.

We met [Edward] Seidensticker just as we entered the temple and stayed with him the whole time. Just inside the genkan [entrance] sat Mrs. Tanizaki and other family members, who greeted us as we entered. We were then shown to a large zashiki [room] where all the guests waited for the ceremony to begin. We had time to take a leisurely look at the company. Seidensticker [hereafter EGS] thoughtfully identified some of the guests:

Takamine Hideko [1924–2010], the actress, looks younger than her age. Pretty, with a round face; poised, pleasant. EGS said that at Tanizaki's funeral, six years ago, she made a fool of herself by talking too much and too tearfully and was upstaged by Kyō Machiko [another actress, b. 1924], who simply laid her flowers on the altar and returned to her seat, calm and dignified.

Kita Morio [1927–2011], novelist, very popular right now. A nice-looking man, a bit heavy in the jowls, gray-black hair, with a solemn, downcast look.

Kon Tōkō [1898–1977], novelist-priest. Looks old, his baldness accentuated by his priestly shave. Jolly ("silly," according to EGS).

Endō Shūsaku [1923–96], novelist, author of *Silence*. Nice looking, young looking. Long, neatly combed black hair, heavy dark-rimmed glasses. He was with a little boy who stared at me happily and curiously.

Kanze Hideo [1927–2007], Mrs. Tanizaki's son-in-law, a member of the great Kanze Noh family. He wore formal kimono and hakama, has a handsome, square face—dignified and masculine.

Takaori Taeko, daughter of Hashimoto Kansetsu, the painter, and mother of Watanabe Chimako [Mrs. Tanizaki's daughter-in-law]. She is a well-known waka poet and a very urbane lady, able to speak English well. Tall and handsome.

Watanabe Seiji, Mrs. Tanizaki's son by her first husband. [Having no children of her own, Matsuko's sister Watanabe Shigeko adopted Seiji.]

"O-haru," the maid who was the model for "Oharu" of *The Makioka Sisters*. She looks fifty-five or so, wears a pink kimono. She *looks* like a maid—good-natured, friendly.

Takeda Ayuko, Tanizaki's only child. She closely resembles her father—round face, a bit resembling the blackened Buddha-head in the Kōfukuji museum. A pleasant, genial smile, bright eyes. EGS remarked that at the age of eighty she'd be a dead ringer for her father.

Tanizaki Seiji [谷崎精二, 1890–1971], one of Jun'ichirō's younger brothers: I caught only a glimpse; he looks very elderly, thin, bald. Another younger brother [Shūhei], makes a rather brown impression; he has a round face and resembles Jun'ichirō more than Seiji does.

All four of the "Makioka" sisters were there. Matsuko [Mrs. Tanizaki] was as always: beautiful and elegant, warm, self-effacing. Shigeko [Yukiko, in the novel] was only just present; as usual, her "shadow was thin." The two I'd not seen before, Asako [who corresponds to Tsuruko in the novel] and Nobuko (Taeko/Koi-san) were much as I expected. Asako looks her age, or more; she's thin to the point of emaciation; her face is boney and somehow dark; but she smiles nicely and slightly resembles Mrs. Tanizaki. As one would expect from the novel, she's a bit too stiff, perhaps inflexible—or is it my imagination? Nobuko was the only sister in Western clothes, a black dress with white polka dots, rather ordinary looking. Her face is ordinary, too—her hair stringy and unkempt, her face heavy and sagging, looking tired and dissipated. She seems to lack completely the grace and elegance of the other three sisters.

Others present included the presidents of [the publishing houses] Kōdansha (a pleasant, big, stately man) and Shinchōsha; Mr. Shimanaka of Chūō Kōron; a large, loud man from the *Mainichi* [newspaper]; and Ibuki Kazuko, Tanizaki's amanuensis.

At 11:15 we were summoned to the main hall for the ceremony. By the time Susan, EGS and I got there, the hall was filled to capacity; for a minute it looked as if we would have to stand outside on the veranda, but people bunched together, so that we managed with some struggle to kneel at the very edge of the room. I was stuck with my feet pressed hard on the door sill and after ten minutes could no longer bear it, and so I moved around to the veranda at the side, where I could stand unobtrusively and see better, as well.

[A sketch I made at the time shows that the room was rectangular, with the main altar and the priests' dais at the west end, Tanizaki's altar at the east end. The dais was decorated with hydrangeas. The family sat along the north side of the room, with Mrs. Tanizaki and Ayuko closest to Tanizaki's altar; the guests, along the south side. Beyond the screens to the north were other rooms; a veranda ran along the southern and eastern sides of the room.]

The ceremony began with a group of priests on a dais, chanting and ceremonially casting large white petals in a graceful, dance-like motion that reminded me of Bugaku dances. The head priest's head-dress was like nothing I'd ever seen before—a bit like a box, a bit like a three-cornered hat, and brown to match his cassock. [I found later that this headwear, called a *suikan* (水冠), is unique to the Jōdo sect.]

The offering of incense followed the priests' performance. Mrs. Tanizaki went first. She stepped elegantly forward as the priests chanted sutras in the background. She moved slowly, formally, gracefully, to the middle of the open space in front of the main altar, bowed to the altar, then to the guests, and then to Tanizaki's altar. She was followed by Ayuko, Tanizaki Seiji, and all the other family members. The incense ceremony began slowly, but the pace quickened gradually until the guests were moving up three, four, and five at a time, waiting their turns. Bowing became more perfunctory, except the bows to Mrs. Tanizaki and Ayuko, who were stationed in front of the family group.

The picture of Tanizaki on the altar was a delight and compensated for the nervousness and inevitable awkwardness of the occasion. [In the photograph,] he was sitting back comfortably in kimono and laughing, with the same twinkle that shows, too, in the collection of photographs 日本の作家 ["Japanese Writers," by Hayashi Tadahiko (林忠彦)].

After kneeling in front of the altar and bowing to the picture, each of us took three pinches of granulated incense and dropped it onto a smoldering mound in a separate bowl. Then another bow to the altar, and a bow to Mrs. Tanizaki and Ayuko.

The sutra chanting ended as the last guest offered incense. Three interesting and beautiful performances followed. Kanze Hideo stood facing Tanizaki's photograph and performed a passage from a Noh play [*Kagekiyo* 景清], a recitative and a few deliberate steps and gestures. He was followed by Inoue Yachiyo, the great dancer and head of the Inoue School. She choreographed the Miyako Odori that Mrs. Tanizaki took us to in April, taught dancing to [Mrs.] Tanizaki's granddaughter [Watanabe Taori], and is a great friend of the Tanizakis. Tiny and gray, proud and dignified, very much the great lady of dance. She performed "Yomigiu" [蓬生], the lyrics of which were written by Tanizaki himself. Two shamisen accompanied her, and the players sang, as well. ["Yomogiu" is the title of the fifteenth chapter of *The Tale of Genji*, translated by EGS as "The Wormwood Patch." Tanizaki's lyrics can be found in the *Complete Works*, 30:293.]

Yachiyo's dance was the high point of the afternoon. The music, slow but tense, sounds more like an echo of music than music itself, and this sensation combines with the slow pace and unearthly melodies and harmonies to produce a haunting effect.

It was too much for Mrs. Tanizaki. She started to weep after a few minutes and for some time was dabbing her eyes with a handkerchief and kimono sleeve.

Kohana (子花), a famous geisha of the Inoue School, performed after her mistress. She is young and classically beautiful; her hair was done in an elaborate, Edo-period style, and she wore a long kimono, purple fading into lavender. She danced "Kosu no to" 小簾の戸.

[I remember that Kon Tōkō, too, played a role, performing a ritual in front of Tanizaki's altar.]

Following the dances, the guests were ushered into a spacious adjoining room, the far wall of which is beautifully painted in weathered golds and browns. Here we were served a makunouchi bentō [boxed] lunch: rice and various vegetables, tofu, and pickles tastefully and artfully arranged in a lacquered box. There was no meat, though there was fish.

I sat next to the only foreigner present other than the two of us and EGS. A silver-haired lady who teaches English at a college in Kyoto, Edith Shiffert. She is a poet, too, and is interested in modern Japanese poetry. She had some harsh comments about certain English translations of Hagiwara. Miss Shiffert was present because of her close friendship with Mrs. Takaori.

Mrs. Tanizaki made appearances for the guests several times in the course of the day. She went from person to person while we waited for the ceremony to begin and spoke to everyone with her usual warmth and charm. She apologized to us for not writing—she intended to, but was just too busy; and she thanked us for the photographs we had sent her.

She was wearing a pale-green silk kimono embroidered with what looked like a maple-leaf pattern. (Considering the season, I suppose they weren't maple leaves, but something similar.) (My diary, 6/30/71)

SEIDENSTICKER'S ACCOUNT OF THE OBSERVANCE OF THE SEVENTH ANNIVERSARY OF TANIZAKI'S DEATH, 1971

The Tanizaki services began in the morning and, with lunch, extended over to mid-afternoon. It was very much as last time: a rather long visit in a large room where no one, save Tony Chambers and I, seemed to be speaking to anyone; and then the chanting and booming and chanting and offering of incense; and three dances by famous people, Kanze Hideo and Inoue Yachiyo and the geisha Kohana (I wonder whether they get paid for these services, or think the honor payment enough); and then lunch. The whole Makioka establishment was there, including O-haru, an exceedingly pleasant woman who must have been just as sweet as o-shiruko in the Makioka days. It is easy to see why Tanizaki preferred the middle sisters. The oldest is all drawn and wizened and looks a good score of years older than Matsuko; and the youngest is, as my mother used to like to say, coarse and vulgar. This last fact perhaps helps to confirm a theory I have long had, that the novel got out of hand, that Tanizaki did not really want Taeko to be so likeable.

At lunch I was seated beside Mr. Shimanaka. Among the celebrities ranged opposite us were Kon Tōkō, Minakami Ben [novelist, 1919–2004; he is also known as Mizukami Tsutomu], Setouchi Harumi [瀬戸内晴美, a novelist who later took Buddhist vows and changed her name to Jakuchō (寂聴), b. 1922], and, substitute for a celebrity, Mrs. Funahashi Seiichi. On Mr. S's other side was Kohana. She seemed silent and sullen, however, and, knowing where the better business lay, quickly moved over to Kon Tōkō, whom she engaged in lively conversation. Let me say again what I said last night: geisha are their own undoing, and one does not feel too dreadfully sad over what is happening to Ponto-chō [a geisha district in Kyoto].

Before coming back to the hotel, we, Miss Ibuki, Chambers, and I . . . paid a visit to the grave, which, when last I saw it, was unfinished. It is very beautiful: white sand, and two natural stones, on one, the Tanizaki plot, in the sensei's writing, the character *jaku* [寂], "quiet," and on the other, the Watanabe plot, in the same hand, *kū* [空], "nothing" or "emptiness." Very beautiful—and at the same time a touch pretentious? Nothing to tell you that it is the great man's grave. You are expected to know. And is it not a little morbid that the two sisters should be so close, and that Mrs. Watanabe should have her new house right across the street from where they are to be buried? I wonder where <u>Mr.</u> Watanabe is buried. Did they dig him up and bring him to Kyoto?

I thought about the Japanese dance. It is much less abstract and so much more mimetic than the Western dance that you have to understand the words to appreciate it. Maybe my trouble is that I have an unfortunate way of missing key words and phrases. (Seidensticker's diary, 6/30/1971, Edward Seidensticker Papers, 7–8, Archives, University of Colorado Boulder Libraries)

I VISIT MRS. TANIZAKI'S HOUSE IN
YUGAWARA, 1973 AND 1977

Mrs. Tanizaki met me at the station. We took a hired car to her home—a large, pleasant house with a Western-style living room that features picture windows, facing south, providing a view of the Izu Peninsula and the ocean. It's not the house in which Tanizaki died, and is only about one-third the size of that one. In the garden were *hagi*, azaleas, weeping cherries, a peach tree, and camellias. (My diary, 7/29/73)

Porcelain cats decorated the entrance hall. Her collection of candle holders was displayed in the living room, on the east wall, under an oil painting of a nude woman by Sekiguchi Shungo [関口俊吾, 1911–2002], dated December, 1953; it was chosen by Tanizaki, she said. On the north wall is a small painting of the Madonna and child by Takabatake [高畠達四郎, 1895–1976?], adapted from Cimabue. Nearby, in a niche on the east wall, is a watercolor of Tanizaki by Yasuda Yukihiko [安田靫彦, 1884–1978].

Mrs. Tanizaki's Buddhist altar: On the left, as you face it, is a photograph of Tanizaki leaning back in his chair, relaxed, grinning. Mrs. Tanizaki said she chose this picture because she didn't want to look at a stern expression every day. On the right, a full-length photo of Watanabe Shigeko. And inside, toward the left, a small, dark, faded photograph of Tanizaki's mother. (Heaps of interesting material lay in front of the altar; she said she has no time to organize it, much less to read it.) (My diary, 7/4/77)

MY ACCOUNT OF AN EVENING AT THE
DISCO WITH MRS. TANIZAKI, 1980

Mrs. Tanizaki saw *Hair* recently and enjoyed it. She also wants to go to a disco, to see what it's like. I urged Robert Campbell to take her (I'd go, too, of course). Maybe Tsubaki House on a Thursday evening. She wants to try anything once, she says. (My diary, 5/11/80)

Met Mrs. Tanizaki at the Hilton Hotel. We had dinner at the Keyaki Grill. She says they have the best food of any Tokyo hotel, and the sort-of-French food we had was excellent: asparagus, the season's special (¥2000 per helping!) and fish—sea bass for her, trout for me. After ordering, she excused herself to make a phone call to her daughter's—and excused herself and excused herself. I kept saying all right; but it turned out that she needed a ten-yen coin to make the call. I gave her three. She wanted to check whether the Kanze grandchildren had come home yet, and, if they had, to urge them to join us for dinner.

After 8:00PM, we met Robert Campbell in the lobby. Feeling sorry for having kept him waiting, we took him some dessert goodies—cake, candy, and an ice cream cube.

The rest of the evening was devoted to Mrs. Tanizaki's first visit to a disco. She has been wanting to go to see what a disco is like, but her grandchildren laughed when she suggested it and wouldn't take her. She was also afraid that too-loud music would affect her heart, and too-cold air-conditioning, her cracked rib; but Robert said that Tsubaki House (in Shinjuku) was not excessively loud, and besides had the advantage of being the most interesting and representative disco, the one where the strangest people gather. In the taxi, she said that she goes out of her way to do things like this so that she can carry the stories (お土産話) to Tanizaki when the time comes, and tell him about everything that has been going on since he died. She also went to see *Hair* with this in mind, she said. Other topics will include foods; space exploration (especially landing on the moon); fashions, such as miniskirts; and [the Kabuki actor] Tamasaburō, who, she thinks, plays the pitiless Tanizaki heroine perfectly. These are all areas that fascinated her husband, she said.

In the elevator lobby, as we waited to go up to Tsubaki House, she asked whether I'd ever been to a gay bar. Yes, I said. She said she'd heard that they treat women very well, that women can relax and have a good time. [I never did take her to one, though it occurred to me later that Maruyama "Miwa" Akihiro's place might have been all right.]

Tsubaki House turned out to be too loud for comfortable conversation, but it didn't seem to bother Mrs. Tanizaki. She seemed rather excited. The young and very courteous boy who greeted us when the elevator doors opened immediately sized us up as an unusual group—two American men with an elderly, elegant Japanese lady. He led us on a circuit of the place and tried to find seats for us. Finally settled at a small table, we ordered lemon squashes. Robert picked up a balloon from among those the employees were inflating as decorations. Blowing it up, he handed it to Mrs. Tanizaki, who toyed with it happily. She observed that it vibrated perceptibly with the music, like a heartbeat, she said.

She said that she used to dance often in Kobe: the tango, jitterbug, and waltz. As she talked, she was getting into the spirit, turning her torso and arms elegantly in time with the music. Robert invited her to dance with him. She hesitated, then accepted. He told me later that she was an excellent dancer, not at all self-conscious, and that anyone who could do the jitterbug could disco-dance with her eyes closed. She was in kimono; instead of flinging her arms about aimlessly, like the youngsters who don't know how to dance, she made Japanese-dance-style movements with her hands, a bit like those in the Awa Odori. The other dancers paused and formed a circle around them, watching in amusement and delight. She laughed happily and said, "They're all having a good time, aren't they" (みんな喜んでいますね). She looked radiant when she came back to the table.

The place is healthy and wholesome (健康的), she said, for these young people (and they were very young, looking like high-school-age kids) to have this outlet (発散); this radiation of youthful energy appealed to her (ひかれます), she said.

She told Robert that when her grandson (Kanze Katsurao) is away from the house, she sometimes puts on his records and dances by herself to keep her legs limber. (My diary, 6/15/80)

MY BIRTHDAY DINNER, JULY 1, 1980

I met Mrs. Tanizaki, Robert [Campbell], Kanze Emiko, her daughter Akome, [and] Akome's friend and her mother, named Ōhashi, for an excellent dinner at the Hilton. During the main course, my chair gradually collapsed under me, giving everyone a good laugh as I sank slowly out of sight. The chair was constructed with a tubular steel frame, thickly upholstered, and provided with arms. Apparently the metal bar against the floor on the left side had a crack and broke when I leaned back. The collapse felt like settling back into a very deep chair. The dining room staff were appalled and insisted that nothing like this had ever happened before. The chairs had supported sumo wrestlers. The waiters were good not to show their amusement, which they must have felt, and the guests were all in hysterics, gasping for breath to ask if I was all right. Mrs. Tanizaki's purse kept falling off her chair, until finally she said, "Everything seems to be falling tonight," which elicited more peals of laughter. (My diary, 7/1/80, and a letter to my parents)

MY ACCOUNT OF DINNER WITH TANIZAKI
MATSUKO AND ICHIDA YAE, 1983

Mrs. Tanizaki was in Kyoto for an exhibit and sale of kimonos and obis inspired by poems she had written. I met her at the exhibition hall, where she also ran into her old friend Ichida Yae. The three of us, plus Mrs. Tanizaki's maid-companion, set out for dinner together. Mrs. Tanizaki asked her driver, Mr. Nakajima, to radio ahead for reservations, but when he did, the restaurant had no room. "We've been jilted!" (ふられた!), Mrs. Tanizaki exclaimed. Mrs. Ichida guided us instead to a tiny restaurant called Kawakami (川上), in Gion. From our small, private room, we could hear the "clock-clock-clock" of wooden clogs outside, a sound from the nineteenth century; and shamisen music drifted in from a house nearby. Mrs. Tanizaki remarked that Tokyo, too, used to sound like this, but today these antique sounds would be drowned out by traffic. People in the next room were conversing in French.

Mrs. Ichida called Mrs. Tanizaki "Matsuko-neechan" [big sister], but she looks much the older. Indeed, she was frail and walked uncertainly with a cane. The stroll of about a block-and-a-half from the car down a narrow lane to the restaurant had so exhausted Mrs. Ichida, leaning on Mr. Nakajima, that she was incapacitated for the first ten minutes; but she took some nitroglycerine to relieve the pain in her arm and soon was back to her usual, droll self. Her cheeks were slack, but when she smiled one could see the charm that must once have been. She talked of Andalusia, Spanish food, and her astonishing hobby, Flamenco. She wants to go to Spain again before she dies, she said, but doesn't think she's strong enough. Mrs. Tanizaki, at eighty, looked youthful beside her.

Mrs. Ichida's hair was dyed raven black, and she was gorgeously dressed. In contrast to Mrs. Tanizaki's subtle kimono—dark lavender, with an almost imperceptible pattern of tiny blossoms or pine needles—Mrs. Ichida's robes were opulent. Her under-kimono, of which one could see about an inch at the neck and lapels, bore a richly embroidered pattern in autumnal shades of brown, gold, yellow, and green; Mrs. Tanizaki's was white. Over this, Mrs. Ichida wore a white kimono with tiny puckers all over it, as if it had been prepared for tie-dying but never dyed. On the shoulders were pale areas of lavender. The effect was one of great extravagance and comfort, almost voluptuousness. On top of her kimono, she wore a knee-length jacket (*uchikake*) in an archaic cut, gorgeously embroidered in autumnal colors. She looked like a large, seventeenth-century doll.

Mrs. Tanizaki told me that Mrs. Ichida is pure Kyoto, from many generations back, but not what one expects from a Kyoto lady. She explained, for instance, why Mrs. Ichida's friends call her "Nijō Castle": She wears kimono all the time, even when she lies down for a nap, with the result that her robes get rumpled, and this puts people in mind of the life-sized figures at the Castle, dressed in seventeenth-century robes that have grown wrinkled and dusty from their many years on display. Mrs. Tanizaki's companion quipped, "You can't very well get angry when someone compares you to a castle."

We dropped off Mrs. Tanizaki at the Fujita Hotel and Mrs. Ichida at her house, near Nanzenji; she gave me her telephone number and invited me to come view her garden sometime. I remarked to Mr. Nakajima, "Mrs. Ichida is an interesting woman, isn't she?" He replied, his voice dark with disapproval, "Yes, and you should have seen her in the old days. She was outrageous." (From a letter to my parents, 11/29/83)

Higuchi Tomimaro told me that it was he who first introduced Ichida Yae to Tanizaki, thinking the author might like to use her in something he wrote; and she, too, hoped that she might appear in one of his works, as Tanizaki Matsuko had appeared in *The Makioka Sisters*. Yae was from a Kyoto merchant family, and in those days [after the war], when goods were scarce, she sold on the black market. She also sang and painted, and had had experience with many men. Tanizaki, who didn't like her very much, exposed her past in *A Strange Tale from East of the Kamo* [鴨東綺譚, 1956, alluding to Kafū's *A Strange Tale from East of the (Sumida) River*, ぼく東綺譚, 1936–37]. Contrary to Mrs. Ichida's hopes, this was not at all the world of the Makioka family. Though Tanizaki told her that he wasn't writing about her, the artist who was illustrating the novel had already sketched her house, and so Tanizaki had no choice but to suspend serialization after only six installments. (My diary, 8/18/77)

With Additional Diary Entries and Excerpts from Letters

TANIZAKI'S LIFE AND PERSONALITY

How tall was Tanizaki?

MATSUKO: Slightly taller than Mrs. Tanizaki [Matsuko], who is 5 *shaku* 1 *sun*, or almost 5′1″ (just under 155 cm); and so Tanizaki was perhaps 5′2″ (157.5 cm). (8/5/79)

MATSUKO: Nomura Shōgo's (野村尚吾) biography of Tanizaki is dramatic and very accurate. (8/20/72)

Did Tanizaki often talk about his mother?

MATSUKO: "All the time" (始終はなしました).

His father?

MATSUKO: Rarely spoke of him. "They often quarreled" (よく喧嘩をしました). (8/4/77)

MATSUKO: Tanizaki hated to be late; he always arrived early. (6/15/80)

YAMAGUCHI MITSUKO: The Tanizaki homes in Kyoto—the house, the garden, servants—reminded one of the Heian court life depicted in scrolls and were quite out of step with postwar Japan. (8/80)

HIGUCHI TOMIMARO: While Tanizaki was working on his first translation [into modern Japanese] of *The Tale of Genji* [in 1936–38], he tried to affect a *Genji* atmosphere in his house, putting up Heian-style blinds (すだれ), candles, and the like. (8/18/77)

YAMAGUCHI MITSUKO: There were always at least three maids in the Tanizaki household. Tanizaki disliked countrified girls; he wanted them to be smart and polished. One member of the Yamaguchi family was even helped in learning French from a Tanizaki maid. Two or three maids were always in attendance in the room, even when guests were present. It was like the Heian court. These attendants didn't *do* anything; they just looked at magazines. During the war, having maids was discouraged; young women were supposed to go work in factories. The Yamaguchis were scolded by the police, and always wondered why the Tanizakis weren't scolded, too. (8/80)

YAMAGUCHI MITSUKO: Mrs. Tanizaki, Watanabe Shigeko, and even the maids were always dressed up. Tanizaki himself wore a subdued (しぶい) dark-gray kimono with an expensive obi and *hakama*, even as everyday wear. Tanizaki didn't like the "smell of everyday life" (生活のにおい), which is why Mrs. Tanizaki always had to wear a kimono. Their life was polite and refined; and Tanizaki was always observing people. (8/80)

YAMAGUCHI MITSUKO: Watanabe Shigeko was in charge of the household—the maids, the menu, and so on. Mrs. Tanizaki did nothing but practice calligraphy and the like. (8/80)

YAMAGUCHI MITSUKO: Tanizaki always addressed his wife in polite language [i.e., with polite verb endings, not よびすて]. "Would you care for some tea?" (ちょっと、ちょっと、お茶でも呑みませんか), he'd say. (8/80)

HIGUCHI TOMIMARO: Tanizaki was punctilious (几帳面): he had a little sign by the front door that said "Writing now" (只今執筆中). When Higuchi visited, Tanizaki would carefully turn over the sign to show the blank side and then turn it back as Higuchi left. (7/27/77)

Higuchi Tomimaro offered two examples of Tanizaki's strong sense of obligation (義理堅い、義理厳しい). The first was when Tanizaki delivered flowers himself, on foot, to Isoda Mataichirō (磯田又一郎, 1909–1998), son of his Gion friend Isoda Taka (磯田多佳, a "literary geisha," 文学芸者 [1879–1945]). She had died during the war, while Tanizaki was in retreat and unable to attend her funeral; but as soon as he returned to Kyoto, he visited Mataichirō (who is also a painter, and a friend of Higuchi's). The second example was that Tanizaki sat for a long time—much longer than expected—at the wake for the Kabuki actor Onoe Kikugorō VI (1885–1949). (7/27/77)

HIGUCHI TOMIMARO: At the same time, Tanizaki could be brusque and intimidating (無愛想、こわい). For example: a certain reporter wanted to meet Tanizaki, but Tanizaki refused. The newspaper urged the reporter to go through Higuchi, since he was a friend and neighbor of Tanizaki's. The reporter pleaded with Higuchi, saying that he couldn't return to the paper without meeting Tanizaki. Higuchi telephoned Tanizaki to explain the situation. Tanizaki agreed to meet the reporter because of Higuchi's intervention; when they arrived, Tanizaki was cheerful and friendly when he spoke to Higuchi, but when he turned to the reporter, he snarled, "Why did you come? I've already told you I don't want to see you." The abashed (恐縮) reporter lacked the courage to say anything, much less to ask any questions. On the way back, Higuchi took pity on him and introduced him to the poet Yoshii Isamu [吉井勇, 1886–1960]. Yoshii sympathized, too. "I'm surprised you went to see that intimidating man" (よくその怖い人のところへ行ったね), he said. (7/27/77)

Mr. Nakajima, Tanizaki's driver, told me a story that illustrates Tanizaki's gruff side. On a late afternoon, when Nakajima was driving Tanizaki from the eastern side of Kyoto to an appointment on the western side, Tanizaki growled, "The sun is in my eyes! (まぶしい！). Take another route!" Nakajima pointed out politely that heading into the sun is unavoidable when one is driving from east to west in the late afternoon. This explanation didn't placate Tanizaki. (11/83)

HIGUCHI TOMIMARO: Once when Tanizaki attended a Noh performance, the actor's undershirt showed from beneath his costume. Tanizaki left the theater angrily. (8/18/77)

HIGUCHI TOMIMARO: Tanizaki didn't say anything lightly (いい加減なことを言わない). (7/27/77)

HIGUCHI TOMIMARO: Tanizaki was honest (正直)—absurdly honest (くそ正直); he always avoided falsehoods. (7/27/77)

SHIGEYAMA SENSAKU: When Sensaku went to visit, Tanizaki would come right out to the front door (玄関) to greet him, but he hated reporters and photographers. (Mrs. Tanizaki agreed: the word was out among reporters that Tanizaki was one to stay away from.) If a reporter came to the door, Tanizaki would bellow, "Who's there! I don't meet with newspaper reporters!" (だれだ！新聞記者にあわないぞ！). He'd never say he was out—he never lied. He'd admit that he was in, but refuse to see them. (7/2/77)

YAMAGUCHI MITSUKO: Tanizaki was childlike, high-strung, cute, wayward, devilish, and well-mannered (子供っぽい、神経質、かわいいらしい、わがまま、悪魔的、礼儀正しい). He could get away with it, being who he was. He was also hard to please (気難しい), and grew more so as he got older. (8/80)

Howard Hibbett said he never saw Tanizaki snap at anyone. "Despite what you may hear from others, he was always amiable and pleasant when I saw him." (5/6/77)

MATSUKO: Tanizaki did what he liked, only associated with people he liked. (8/5/79)

YAMAGUCHI KŌICHI: Tanizaki was a loner (一匹狼) and avoided others (交際がない) because interacting with them was too much trouble (面倒臭い). Confident in himself, he wouldn't allow any interference with his time. (8/13/77)

YAMAGUCHI KŌICHI: Tanizaki was a rationalist (合理主義者). "I am myself; what others do is nothing to me" (自分は自分、人が何をしていても僕には関係ない). "I take care of myself" (自分を大切にする). "I know my own failings, but I don't compare myself with others and try to correct my failings" (自分の欠点が分かっていても他人との比較に向いてそれを改めようとしない). "I'm fine the way I am" (これでいいのだ、おれは). This, according to Yamaguchi, was Tanizaki's attitude. He was true to himself (自分に忠実). He examined himself (反省はあった), but even though he did have failings, he was himself (欠点があっても僕は僕だ). And he could be cold (つめたい)—not cold to Yamaguchi, but he maintained a distance between his own interests and everything else. (8/13/77)

YAMAGUCHI KŌICHI: Tanizaki broke out of the standard view of history and went beyond the conventional interpretations. He was, said Yamaguchi, an unconventional, original person (型はずれで独創的), one who could easily detach himself from Japanese sensibility (日本人の感覚から簡単に出られる人). (8/13/77)

Yamaguchi Kōichi said he learned from Tanizaki to look at things without preconceptions or prejudice. Tanizaki looked at everything

with fresh eyes. For example, though the tradition of the tea ceremony has had a profound influence on the way people look at antiques, Tanizaki saw antiques for what they were, not for how they'd
been appraised by a tea master or for how they conformed to a conventional set of aesthetics. (8/13/77)

MATSUKO: Tanizaki had a good eye for antiques but no interest in
collecting them. He collected ukiyoe before the earthquake, but
not after. (7/4/77)

MATSUKO: Tanizaki was always curious. Though not a baseball fan,
he took Mrs. Tanizaki to see Babe Ruth at Kōshien Stadium, in
Osaka [in 1934]. He also went to see Johnny Weismuller, the
Zeppelin, and an aviator named Smith [probably the WWI ace
James Robert Smith]. (8/17/85)

MATSUKO: Tanizaki loved everything new, and loved science fiction
movies. (2/22/80)

MATSUKO: Tanizaki and Western languages: Tanizaki could speak
English pretty well when he lived in Yokohama and always continued to read English. (summer 1980)

MATSUKO: He was confident of his ability to read English, but had
difficulty with listening comprehension, especially when the
speaker had an accent. A Spanish photographer came around
toward the end to take Tanizaki's picture (it was delivered after
his death). Tanizaki couldn't understand the man's English and
had Emiko (Mrs. Tanizaki's daughter) translate for him. He studied German at Tokyo University, and regretted that he couldn't
read French. "There are so many things I'd like to read," he'd say:
Balzac, Radiguet, Stendhal. He read *The Japan Times* [in English]
and considered it the most accurate and detailed of Japanese
newspapers. (7/4/77)

Diabetes?

MATSUKO: He had it from his early years, but it was never serious, and in later years it disappeared. He never needed medication for diabetes or a special diet. When he was examined for high blood pressure (in the late 1940s) there was no longer any trace of diabetes. (7/4/77)

MATSUKO: In the late 1920s he had thought he'd like to live in Osaka (すきなまちでございまして)—Doshōmachi, Kōraibashi— quiet, the old Semba area. But Osaka changed rapidly, and Tanizaki's affections switched to Kyoto. He especially liked the food in Kyoto and Osaka. (7/4/77)

Donald Keene vividly recalled seeing Tanizaki as he left the Fukudaya, in Tokyo, "moving in a cloud of women"—Matsuko, Shigeko, and maids. He had the impression that Tanizaki "didn't enjoy the company of men, except perhaps some of his old friends and classmates." Keene also remembers Tanizaki returning to the Fukudaya bright and happy, "like a little boy," pleased with the shoes he'd bought. The maids at the inn were amused, because they could see how cheaply made the shoes were, but Tanizaki "didn't know about such things." (5/9/77)

YAMAGUCHI MITSUKO: Tanizaki didn't care to have men or boys around, but women were all right, even if they were journalists. The only boys who were free to come and go were Seiji [Mrs. Tanizaki's son] and Mrs. Yamaguchi's son, Akira. Even the cats were female. Tanizaki never hired houseboys. "Literary youths" (文学青年) would come around, but Tanizaki refused to see them. Feeling sorry for them, Mrs. Tanizaki would feed them. (8/80)

MATSUKO: Everyone said that Tanizaki was very broad in his interests and perspective, and had *hōyōryoku* (包容力, magnanimity, broad-mindedness, tolerance). On his lack of prejudices: Once

Emiko entered into marriage discussions with a shoe dealer from the fashionable Ginza district. Mrs. Tanizaki hesitated because of what people would think (most people in the shoe business being members of the *burakumin* community, who are often discriminated against), but Tanizaki responded, "What difference does that make? I don't understand that nonsense. Don't say stupid things" (何それや違うもんか？ そんなのは分からない！ 馬鹿なことを言うな！). When? 23 years ago—i.e., 1954. (7/4/77)

MATSUKO: Tanizaki had friendly feelings (好意) for foreigners and held no prejudices against them, even toward Koreans. He had great respect for China: "Everything came from China, didn't it?" He often talked about China's great antiquity—a culture from thousands of years ago, much older than Japan's. The Heian period was an exception, of course—a uniquely Japanese culture, in contrast to the Sinified Nara period; and Tanizaki said, in so many words, that he liked the Heian period best in Japanese history. Why? For its atmosphere (情緒) and elegance (風致). He liked the language of the *Genji* and admired Murasaki Shikibu's ability in Sino-Japanese (漢文). (7/4/77)

MATSUKO: Tanizaki never told his wife anything about dealing with publishers, copyrights, royalties, and the like. When publishers came to talk business, Tanizaki would shoo her out of the room. It has taken her years to get the hang of it. (8/4/77)

Marriages

Higuchi Tomimaro said he met Nezu Seitarō [Mrs. Tanizaki's first husband and the model for Kei-boy in *The Makioka Sisters*] in about 1921, before Nezu married Matsuko. Nezu had bought one of Higuchi's paintings and invited Higuchi to his home. Not at all what Higuchi expected in an art collector, Nezu was young and looked like a university student. He lived in a huge house with his grandmother and servants. His mother had died when he was born; his father put him off on the grandmother, who reared him carefully, forbidding him to play with boys who might be a bad influence. She considered Higuchi to be a good influence and invited him to visit now and then. Nezu lived in great luxury and was extravagant—he even had an automobile for leisure, when very few men had one even for business. His neighbors held a low opinion of him and early on predicted that his fortune would collapse, because of his ostentatiousness and because all his visitors were geisha and artists.

Through Nezu, Higuchi met Matsuko and later met Tanizaki.

Nezu was loose (だらしない), he said, referring to Nezu's relationship with Matsuko's youngest sister, Nobuko [信子, model for Koi-san/Taeko, in *The Makioka Sisters*]. He surmises that Matsuko was not without feelings of revenge (復讐の気持ち) when she took up with Tanizaki. Once in the late 1940s Mrs. Tanizaki was paged at the Minamiza Theater, in Kyoto. Going out to the lobby, she discovered that Nezu had come to ask for money (こずかい). Mita Jun'ichi [三田純市, 1923–1994] has written on the life of Nezu, drawing on Higuchi's recollections [in 『道頓堀物語』, 1978?]. (7/27/77)

MATSUKO: Chiyo [Tanizaki's first wife] was too domestic (家庭的) for Tanizaki's liking. He lost interest in her (だれてしまった). Tomiko [his second wife] was not domestic enough, and Tanizaki was disillusioned/disappointed (失望) after marrying her. She was more like a female houseboy-student (女書生) than a wife. Tanizaki said, "I completely misread her. It was my fault" (すっかり見違えていた。わるかった). In other words, she didn't turn out as Tanizaki expected. She was useful as a secretary, but not as a wife—as a companion at the theater, for example. It was always like taking a student along with him. She lacked atmosphere, spirit (情調), and was open, uncomplicated (さっぱりして). (8/4/77)

MATSUKO: The first time Matsuko met Tanizaki alone (as opposed to meeting him in a group, such as with Nezu), he asked, "Do you like *uta*?" (うたがお好きですか). Thinking he meant singing (*uta*), she replied, "No, I can't" (いいえ、できません). He responded, "I'm talking about *waka*" [Japanese poetry, sometimes called *uta*] (和歌のことですよ). She replied that yes, she liked *waka* very much. He was delighted; he took *waka* seriously. After the war, in Atami, he took her to study poetry with [the scholar-poet] Sasaki Nobutsuna [佐佐木信綱, 1872–1963]; it would be better for her to work with a real expert than for him to check her poems himself, he said. She worked with Sasaki for fifteen years, until he told her, "There's nothing for me to correct any more" (もう直すところはありません). (12/30/86)

HIGUCHI TOMIMARO: Tanizaki asked Higuchi to paint a portrait of Matsuko in order to make a good impression on her. The portrait of Chacha in the first edition of *A Blind Man's Tale* [盲目物語, 1931] was painted by Kitano Tsunetomi [北野恒富, 1880–1947], Higuchi's mentor. [Matsuko was the model for this portrait.] (8/18/77)

MATSUKO: In 1930–32 Tanizaki already had Matsuko in his heart, though she was not aware of it yet. She has been asked why he took a detour (回り道) to Matsuko, via Tomiko, instead of going directly from Chiyo to Matsuko. First of all, Tanizaki was modest (謙虚) and diffident (つつましい), and thought that Matsuko was too high for him, "a flower blossoming on a high peak, a blossom he could not pluck" (高峰の花、折れもしない花).

Tanizaki insisted that he never misled Tomiko (だましたことはない). There were too many obstacles around Matsuko—her husband, her children—and marrying her seemed out of the question at the time. Why remarry at all, after divorcing Chiyo? Because he was lonely in 1930, seeing Chiyo and Satō Haruo so happy together.

When Tanizaki married Tomiko, he didn't have her name officially entered in his family register (入籍), but when it became clear that they would separate, Tomiko insisted that he do so. After the separation, Tanizaki told Matsuko that they must look after Tomiko; if they didn't, it would cast a shadow over Tanizaki's and Matsuko's relationship. Matsuko sold most of her belongings, even mementos from her parents, to raise money to help Tomiko. Tomiko was bitter (うらむ) toward Matsuko, not toward Tanizaki. She thought that Matsuko tricked (だました) Tanizaki and called her a *tanuki* [raccoon-dog, often translated "badger"; like foxes, *tanuki* are sometimes thought to use magical powers to enchant men]. (8/4/77)

MATSUKO: "We resolved to commit lovers-suicide if our marriage didn't work out" (結婚がうまく行かなければ心中の約束をしました). This was Mrs. Tanizaki's response when her granddaughter (Kanze Akome) remarked that Mrs. Tanizaki needed courage to leave Nezu and marry Tanizaki. It wouldn't be such a big deal now, she said, but in the 1930s it was a serious matter. Mrs. Tanizaki's response was intended to show how seriously she and Tanizaki took it. (4/18/80)

Did Tanizaki change in early Showa [late 1920s to early 1930s; we asked because many readers see a change in his writing at that time]?

MATSUKO: Yes. Before his relationship with Mrs. Tanizaki, he would sleep until after noon and work until dawn. When he started living with Matsuko, he stopped working at night and got up early in the morning. He changed his schedule because otherwise he'd never see her—she'd be up while he was asleep, and vice versa. As a result of the change, his health improved markedly. He would get up at 7:30, breakfast at 8:00; lunch at 12:00; nap after lunch, and dine at 6:00 exactly. He'd complain if meals were even one minute late. At other times he isolated himself in his study;

Mrs. Tanizaki stayed out except for very urgent matters. After dinner he'd watch television and chat with the family. He especially enjoyed word games (言葉の遊び). When he changed his schedule, he did so abruptly, with no apparent difficulty. He went directly to sleep as soon as he hit the pillow (パタンきゅう). Mrs. Tanizaki, in contrast, has trouble getting to sleep at night and is slow to get started in the morning. (7/4/77)

Higuchi Tomimaro recalled witnessing Tanizaki serving meals to Mrs. Tanizaki when they were living together but before they were married. Maids would bring the food to the kitchen door, where Tanizaki would receive it and serve it to his wife. She did nothing. As she ate, Tanizaki, wearing *jimbei*, would fan her with an *uchiwa* [a round fan]. If he fanned too vigorously, she'd say "Too strong!" (きつい). Tanizaki would eat later, by himself. It was, he said, very much like the relationship between Sasuke and Shunkin, in *A Portrait of Shunkin* [春琴抄, 1933]. This was a sign of her theatricality (芝居気), and was beyond what most women would have tolerated. (7/27/77, 8/18/77)

HIGUCHI TOMIMARO: Tanizaki washed Matsuko's underwear himself. Normally the maids would have washed them, but Tanizaki used the time to think about his writing. (8/18/77)

YAMAGUCHI KŌICHI: When they went to the beach, Tanizaki, wearing a straw hat (麦わら帽子), would carry all the baggage. He was practicing the role of Sasuke serving Shunkin. Mrs. Tanizaki was able to respond in kind when Tanizaki played roles this way. (4/19/78)

Mrs. Tanizaki herself used the word "shibaigi" [芝居気, theatricality] and admitted she couldn't have kept up with Tanizaki without it (なければついていけない). (4/18/80)

HIGUCHI TOMIMARO: At the home of a friend, Senoo Kentarō, Mrs. Tanizaki acted like any other housewife. When she was with Tanizaki, she had to play a role, but at Senoo's she could satisfy herself by doing the womanly chores she couldn't do at home. (8/18/77)

MATSUKO: Tanizaki said that a writer had to be careful what he wrote about his wife. If not, she might end up badly (悪妻), as in the cases of Natsume Sōseki and Dostoyevsky, who didn't get along with his [first] wife [Maria]. Mrs. Tanizaki believes that Tanizaki wrote 雪後庵夜話 ["Nocturnal Musings at Setsugoan", 1963–64] to clear up or avoid misunderstandings about Mrs. Tanizaki. (7/10/78)

On World War II

MATSUKO: "Great nations don't collapse" (大国は滅びない), Tanizaki said, referring to China, the U. S., and the Soviet Union. "Of course we'll lose. We've got to accept that" (負けるに決まっている。その覚悟でいなくてはならない). He was utterly opposed to the war and detested (だいきらい) writers who supported it. The neighborhood brigade (隣組) in Sumiyoshi had a bucket relay. Mrs. Tanizaki was supposed to participate but always got out of it on one excuse or another (いつも逃げました). Finally unable to refuse any longer, she went, wearing mompe [baggy workpants]. Tanizaki was furious and came out to take her home (迎えにきました). "This is stupid! Stop it!" (馬鹿な！ やめてくれ！). He compared the difference between Japan and the U. S. to the difference between a rickshaw and an airplane. (7/4/77)

MATSUKO: "I hope they [the Japanese forces] lose soon" (早く負けてほしい), Tanizaki said. Even becoming subordinate to the

U. S. would be preferable to life under a Japanese military government. He was anti-military because he wanted and needed the freedom to write whatever he wanted. She used the word "freedom" (自由主義) several times. (4/18/80)

What did Tanizaki say about the destruction of Osaka and Tokyo during the war?

MATSUKO: Nothing. (7/4/77)

YAMAGUCHI KŌICHI: Tanizaki disliked the *Man'yōshū* [万葉集, the eighth-century anthology of poetry]. In the nationalistic education of prewar Japan, especially from 1930 on, the collection was extolled as a pure, straightforward, unadorned expression of the Japanese spirit. Scholars emphasized the poets' protestations of loyalty to the emperor and maintained that this was the only *true* poetry. Tanizaki considered it countrified (田舎もん的). He preferred the *Kokinshū* [古今集, 905], for the feeling and logic (理屈) of its poetry; and liked the *Shinkokinshū* [新古今集, 1205] best of all, for the decorativeness and circumlocutions of its poetry. (8/13/77)

YAMAGUCHI KŌICHI: As soon as he arrived in Kyoto after the war, Tanizaki spread a cloth over an orange crate and started writing. (4/19/78)

Fears

MATSUKO: Tanizaki was terrified of earthquakes, even before the great earthquake of 1923. Once there was a tremor in Tokyo when he was staying with Kon Tōkō and Kon's mother. Tanizaki rushed into Mrs. Kon's room, gasping, "What shall I do! What shall I do!" (どうしよう！ どうしよう！). Years later, Tanizaki would bolt out of the house when he felt an earthquake, leaving Mrs. Tanizaki and everyone else behind (私を置いて先に庭へ跳んで行きました). (7/4–5/77)

TANIZAKI AYUKO, MATSUKO, AND SHŪHEI: He was also afraid of power failures. When a typhoon threatened, he would go to a hotel that had its own generator so there'd be no fear of a power outage. (7/12/77)

TANIZAKI AYUKO, MATSUKO, AND SHŪHEI: He was terrified of disease. He took to bed at the first sign of a cold and used to carry water around with him (sugared?), Ayuko recalled. Mrs. Tanizaki didn't remember that. When her children, Seiji and Emiko, had scarlet fever, Mrs. Tanizaki nursed them. Her husband was so afraid that she'd transfer it to him, he made her sleep in his study while he slept in the main house. When Tanizaki invited Shūhei to an anniversary of their parents' death, Shūhei replied that he had a bit of a cold (かぜぎみ) but would attend anyway. A telegram arrived immediately from Tanizaki: "You needn't come" (クルニオヨバズ). But Shūhei had anticipated this; he had recovered by the specified day and went anyway. (7/12/77)

TANIZAKI SHŪHEI: Tanizaki disliked barbershops. Shūhei speculated that a rickshaw carrying Tanizaki once fell backwards, just as a barber chair reclines when you get a shave, and he hit his head. In any case, he never went to a barber; Mrs. Tanizaki cut his hair for him; when he was a child, his mother cut it. (7/12/77)

Religion

MATSUKO: Tanizaki disliked the Nichiren sect, with which his family was affiliated. He preferred Tendai, whose ceremonies he liked, along with its association with the Heian period. He developed a particularly deep interest in Tendai from 1947 on. He wanted, however, to be buried at Hōnen'in, a Jōdo (Pure Land) temple. He originally planned to have all the rituals performed at a Tendai temple, in Tendai style, and Hōnen'in agreed to this. To insist that Hōnen'in perform Tendai ceremonies for him would have been asking too much; but when he witnessed the Hōnen'in rites, he found them admirably old-fashioned and loved the flowers in the main hall. The head priest at Hōnen'in said they could conduct his funeral even if Tanizaki didn't join the Jōdo sect. Tanizaki decided not to insist on Tendai ceremonies. "They put on a good show at Hōnen'in, too" (法然院も演出がいい). (7/4/77, 8/4/77)

MATSUKO: Tanizaki chose their gravestones at the Kamo River, with Mrs. Tanizaki, and designed the plot himself. Planting a weeping cherry tree between the stones was his idea; the tree came from the garden of the Heian Shrine. (7/4/77)

MATSUKO: Tanizaki held the ceremony marking the 33rd anniversary of his mother's death at Manshuin [1949?]. He insisted on doing it in the old way, and it had to be a Tendai ceremony (天台でなければならない). He had the priests perform a ceremony called Hokke Hakkō (法華八講) in the old, Heian style. It was extremely impressive: priests in elaborate robes sang the *Lotus Sutra* in a chorus, with high and low parts, while they scattered pieces of paper in the shape of lotus petals and dyed in various colors—gold, silver, and red. (This scattering of blossoms is called *sange* [散華]. She thinks that in ancient times real petals were used.) The priests say "shinkeirei" (心敬礼) as an *aizu* [合図, signal or cue] during the ceremony. (8/4/77) [The ceremony is mentioned in Chapter 10 ("Sakaki" 賢木) of Murasaki Shikibu's *The Tale of Genji*, where it's called *mi-hakō* (御八講): "Her Majesty (Fujitsubo) was variously occupied with preparations for her Rite of the Eight Discourses" (Tyler's translation, 210).]

MATSUKO: "I have no religion," Tanizaki said. "I'm with Einstein" (自分は信仰がない、アインシュタインと一緒だ). Einstein said that his religion was the universe (宇宙が信仰だ). Tanizaki agreed: "I don't believe in anything else" (ほかに何も信じない). (8/4/77)

Old Age

Shūhei recalled that Tanizaki grew more kind and gentle (やさしい) toward his close relatives as he got older. "He's gotten old" (年を取ったな), thought Shūhei at the time. They all (Mrs. Tanizaki, Ayuko, Shūhei) agreed that before he grew old Tanizaki was brusque (無愛想) with people who were close to him. This is reflected in *In the Style of a Modern Storyteller* [當世鹿もどき, 1961]. Tanizaki's father, Kuragorō, was brusque, too, especially to his children, and so is Shūhei. This is why Tanizaki used a special language to talk with Emiko. Ayuko and Shūhei chuckled over memories of grim, silent meals with Tanizaki—silent because there was nothing to talk about. (7/12/77)

Ibuki Kazuko (Tanizaki's former secretary and amanuensis) once said to me that Tanizaki had told her, in 1960, that if he were stronger he might participate in demonstrations of the sort mentioned in *Diary of a Mad Old Man* [瘋癲老人日記, 1961]. Mrs. Tanizaki was surprised to hear this from me. She thought that Ibuki must misremember. She conceded that Tanizaki detested Kishi Nobusuke (Prime Minister at the time)—disliked his face, said he was no good. (He could judge people by their faces, she said.) But surely he didn't really mean it when he said he might have joined in a demonstration. He probably just threw off the comment lightly, if he said it at all, out of a wish that he were stronger. (4/18/80)

HOWARD HIBBETT: Tanizaki's friends, at least in later life, were "solid citizens," like Mr. Tsuchida of the Dai-ichi Hotel, rather than literary types. (5/6/77)

MATSUKO: During the last year of his life, Tanizaki seemed to sense that he hadn't long to live. At times he seemed lost in thought (考え込んでいるような時) and often wept when talking about the old days or when seeing old friends. Then he'd say, "When you get like this, death isn't far away" (こういうことになると死ぬことは近いんだよ). Shiga Naoya, who was older than Tanizaki, asked Mrs. Tanizaki if her husband ever talked about death. He did, and had mixed feelings: on the one hand, he said, "If I die, I'll have no more cares" (死ねば何もかも安楽になる); on the other, he was afraid of pain (苦痛の恐怖). Later, Shiga himself had his IVs [intravenous injections] stopped and died within two or three days. (7/4/77)

MATSUKO: The day before he died, Tanizaki tried to get up, crying, "I'll die if I stay here. I'm going to Tokyo. I'm going to Tokyo" (ここにいると死んでしまう。東京まで行く、東京まで行く). He called for his wallet and walking stick. "There's more to write before I die" (死ぬ前に書かなければならないものがある). (8/11/79)

EDWARD SEIDENSTICKER: "I used to think Tanizaki was very unlike his work, but now I think he *was* rather like his work. He had a childlike, sweet quality. He didn't talk much, and let Mrs. Tanizaki talk as much as she wanted. He was also very demanding and perhaps unfeeling [of Miss Ibuki]. I was very fond of Tanizaki; he was more approachable than Kawabata." (1989)

Howard Hibbett, in contrast, recalled that Tanizaki talked freely and "a good deal" on all sorts of subjects. Hibbett "never had the impression that Tanizaki was not holding up his end of the conversation." (5/6/77)

HOWARD HIBBETT: Tanizaki was "amiability and affability itself" and was not stiff like some other writers, such as Ishikawa Jun [石川淳, 1899–1987]. (5/6/77)

TANIZAKI'S HABITS AND TASTES

MATSUKO: Tanizaki said he couldn't concentrate in a big room, but he didn't set a wicket or screen around his desk, as Kanzaburō [十七代目中村勘三郎, 1909–1988] did in the stage version of *Peace in the Kitchen* [台所太平記, 1963, translated as *The Maids*]. He worked regularly, like an office worker, 9 to 5, with a break at lunch. He wrote an average of three pages a day. Why so little? He chose his words carefully. He allowed no interruptions. (7/24/76)

Looking out over the ocean from her house at Yugawara, Mrs. Tanizaki recalled that Tanizaki said, in his late years, that he couldn't write in a place without a view of the sea (海の見えないところでは仕事ができない). (7/4/77)

MATSUKO: Tanizaki liked to concentrate while working, without interruptions; but between projects, he enjoyed travel and other diversions to clear his head and get ready to concentrate on the next project. (1/17/83)

Where did Tanizaki like to go for entertainment?

MATSUKO: When he had guests, to Ichiriki [一力, in Kyoto]. But his favorite geisha restaurant was Yoshihatsu (吉初), near the Kaburenjo, in Kyoto; and his favorite geisha there was Okuyama Hatsuko, who now runs a boarding house for students in Ichijōji. (7/4/77)

MATSUKO: Tanizaki said that Hatsuko was the last of the real Gion geisha. (8/4/77)

MATSUKO: Tanizaki enjoyed sitting in the kitchen at Yoshihatsu, watching the bustle of people coming and going. (8/4/77)

A piece of Tanizaki's calligraphy hung on the wall at Yoshihatsu: 紫花緑香 ["purple blossoms green fragrance"]. (7/30/77)

Okuyama Hatsuko said she was born in a Gion restaurant (茶屋) run by her mother. Normally, training (お稽古) began on June 6th of the child's sixth year. Usually a girl would become an apprentice *geiko* [i.e., a *maiko*, 舞子] in her eleventh year, but Hatsuko was late, waiting until she was thirteen (1922). Becoming a *maiko* was her own idea (自分から舞子になりたかった). The process was very expensive, and it was a great distinction for parents to have their daughter become a *maiko*. In Kyoto, one always says *geiko*, not *geisha*. (7/30/77)

Hatsuko thinks it was through the introduction of the writer Kume Masao [久米正雄, 1891–1952] that she first met Tanizaki. She's sharp, talkative, outspoken, elegant and vulgar at the same time, sensual. In her elegant moments, she resembles Mrs. Tanizaki (and says she's been told that). She's not afraid to say clearly what she thinks. Witty and poised, she holds herself and her hands elegantly; but she's likely to jump up like a little girl, say "time to pee!" (おしっこ！), and hurry off to the bathroom. (7/30/77)

Hatsuko said that her dialect was so pure that linguists at Kyoto University made recordings of her speech. (7/30/77)

OKUYAMA HATSUKO: Yamaguchi Kōichi told Hatsuko that he had asked Mrs. Tanizaki whether she thought Tanizaki had had a physical relationship with Hatsuko. "Probably not with Hatsuko-san" (初子さんとはないでしょう), he quoted her as saying. (7/30/77)

Yamaguchi Kōichi said he asked Tanizaki the same question. "I thought about it" (そんな気はあったが), Tanizaki replied, but he lost interest because so many of the men she had been with—Yoshii Isamu, for example—were friends of his. Tanizaki didn't have much physical contact with geisha. (8/13/77)

MATSUKO: Tanizaki hated small handwriting and told the children to write big. "When you write small, you become a small person" (人間も小さくなる). (7/4/77)

MATSUKO: Tanizaki would decide suddenly, literally overnight, to move. Chūō Kōron would help with his belongings, but the maids, who had to pack their own things and the kitchen supplies, were thrown into a panic. At the time of his last move—to Yoshihama [in Yugawara]—he was so impatient, he moved in before the electricity and plumbing were ready and there was no furniture yet; they had to eat on apple crates; but he'd rather put up with anything than to wait two or three days. (8/5/79)

MATSUKO: Why did he move so often? For a change of mood—to keep on writing—so he wouldn't stagnate. He kept a few favorite pieces of furniture and sold all the rest each time he moved. Most of his luggage consisted of books. (7/4/77)

MATSUKO: Tanizaki wanted to go to Europe; also, in later years, he wanted to go to Peking to see old friends like Guo Moruo [郭沫若, 1892–1978], whom he had known well. (7/4/77, 7/10/78) When he lived in Honmoku [in Yokohama, 1922–23] he had a completely Western-style house: he left his shoes on inside, had a Western maid, ate Western food, and went to dance parties. (7/4/77)

MATSUKO: In postwar Japan, Tanizaki was completely indifferent (無関心) to politics—in the prewar period, too, for that matter. He never voted—not once—and politics was another world (別の世界). (7/4/77)

MATSUKO: Tanizaki liked women who looked like cats—petite (すん ずまり), short, with a flat nose; not the standard beauty (美人), but cute (かわいい), with a flat face. (7/4/77)

MATSUKO: He liked cats' willfulness and their resemblance to women (気ままで、女に似ているところが好き). Dogs were uncomplicated, uninteresting (単純で面白くない). He liked people best of all: "I don't like to be in a place with no people" (人間の 居るところでないと嫌だよ), he said. Of course he appreciated nature, but he was more interested in people. (7/4/77)

MATSUKO: A Persian cat, a favorite of Tanizaki's, would wait by his seat at the table for dinner to begin. Tanizaki would give it choice pieces of sashimi, making the maids jealous. But if one of the maids, or anyone else, was mean to the cat, the cat would tell on them, going to Tanizaki and meowing plaintively. When the cat died, Tanizaki had it taken to the Ueno Zoo to be stuffed. Mrs. Tanizaki still has it, in its glass case, but keeps it put away because it's frightening to look at. (8/5/79)

MATSUKO: When Tanizaki was with his dog, he always had cookies in his pocket, because the dog liked them. One dog, a chow chow, wouldn't leave the house after Tanizaki died and Mrs. Tanizaki had moved. Another dog, a collie (or was it a sheep dog?) they had received from the Agriculture Ministry, wept when told that Tanizaki had died, and then died soon after him. (8/5/79)

MATSUKO: Tanizaki loved movies, especially those with contemporary settings (現代もの). He didn't especially enjoy historical pieces (時代もの). His interest in movies didn't end with Taishō Katsuei [the studio for which he wrote screenplays in 1920–21]. In old age, he said that if he had the strength he would like to write and direct his own films. His novels are more adaptable to film than to stage, he said, and he lamented that film directors had not taken advantage of the medium to capture elements of his fiction that would be impossible on stage—fantasy, for example (幻想的な物が好きでございまして). (7/4/77)

MATSUKO: What was it about Osaka that appealed to Tanizaki? He was looking for something not to be found in Tokyo women (東京の女にないものを求めていた), who are coldhearted (情なし). He also disliked the way Tokyo women talk (ものの言い方も嫌いだった). Mrs. Tanizaki also thinks that the Low City (下町) of Tokyo is closer in spirit to Osaka than the High City (山の手): Tanizaki may have felt some affinity between Osaka and the Tokyo of his childhood.

Mrs. Tanizaki says there's a big difference between Tokyo and Osaka people: Tokyoites are obstinate, standoffish, and unyielding (いじっぱり、つめたい、かちき); the rich don't give money to artists without a good, logical reason; they're rigid. Osakans, in contrast, are warm-hearted—they have passion (情) and heart (こころ): the rich impulsively give money to artists. Her first husband was a good example of the Osaka type. At the time of his funeral, the newspapers referred to him as "the last Semba *bonbon*" [船場の最後のボンボン, young son of a rich family, in the Osaka dialect]. Tanizaki didn't understand him or appreciate him until then. Osakans are generous, emotional, passionate (情熱っぽい). Osakans will invite a person to stay with them without hesitation; a Tokyo man will grumble, "Why should I?" (そんな筋合いがない). (8/5/79)

MATSUKO: Tanizaki enjoyed shopping at the Nishiki market, in Kyoto. (8/5/79)

MATSUKO: Tanizaki's likes and dislikes in maids were extreme. He'd favor some with gifts, ignore others, even ask that they not be allowed to be near him (よこさないでください), and if he passed one he disliked in the hallway, he'd turn away and avoid her. There were no particular reasons for his likes and dislikes, and when a disliked maid tried to make a good impression on him, he'd only dislike her more. Those he liked, he would take on outings, and the course was always the same: a movie, then tea, then shopping for a purse or necklace. (8/5/79)

MATSUKO: Tanizaki always carried his brief case with him, setting it between his feet in a taxi, for instance. It was old and tattered, an example of his habit of using a thing until it was completely worn out. (8/5/79)

MATSUKO: Tanizaki liked to read mysteries, including those of Agatha Christie. He was close to Edogawa Rampo [writer, 1894–1965] before he married Matsuko, but not after. (12/30/86)

Would Tanizaki have met and talked with me?

MATSUKO: Of course—he was punctilious about such things. (12/29/82)

Food and Drink

MATSUKO: Tanizaki used to say that he couldn't write if he didn't have delicious food. (8/5/79)

Higuchi Tomimaro had the impression that Tanizaki began looking forward to the day's meals the moment he woke up. (7/27/77)

One of Mrs. Tanizaki's maids told me that, at lunch, Tanizaki would go over a list of what fish were available from the market that day and order dinner accordingly. (8/4/77)

HOWARD HIBBETT: Tanizaki had "a great zest for food" and "ate with great relish," even in his last years. He was especially fond of *hamo* [an eel]. Mrs. Tanizaki, concerned about his drinking, would often say "Don't you think you've had enough beer"? (5/6/77)

MATSUKO: While eating sukiyaki, another person will sometimes take the meat one has put in the pan oneself. Tanizaki would spit on his finger and touch his own pieces of meat, saying, "This is mine!" (これは僕のだ！) (4/18/80)

MATSUKO: Tanizaki liked Chinese and French food when he was young, but when he grew older he preferred Japanese food. Chinese food all tastes the same, he said. Japanese food brings out the real flavor of good ingredients; French food is all sauces and seasonings. (8/5/79)

MATSUKO: In later years Tanizaki said that when he ate Chinese food his stomach felt like a garbage dump (ごみため). All Chinese food is the same [he said]—fried in a skillet—and you just toss it into the dump. Mrs. Tanizaki once told this story to Maruya Saiichi in a conversation for publication (対談) and then tried to retract it, because they didn't want to embarrass their Chinese friends. In particular, she was mindful of the chef at Hiun (飛雲), one of Tanizaki's favorite Chinese restaurants (in Kiyamachi [Kyoto], near the Muse coffee house), who was so fond of Tanizaki that he went to Tanizaki's grave every July 30th after his death. (7/4/77)

MATSUKO: Tanizaki ate fast—a holdover from his days as a student. He was so partial to Kyoto cuisine—and they believed it was good for him—that Mrs. Tanizaki regularly took Kyoto food to him when he was in the hospital. She's convinced it's the healthiest. (fall 1983)

MATSUKO: When he was living at Yugawara, Tanizaki sometimes ordered food from Kyoto by air freight. The actress Naniwa Chieko, whose family made Saga tofu, would bring some with her whenever she went from Kyoto to Tokyo. Mrs. Tanizaki would wait at the Atami station, and Naniwa would drop off the tofu. Tanizaki also ordered *mabuna* [*Carassius cuvieri*] and *hamo* from Kyoto. (7/4/77)

YAMAGUCHI MITSUKO: Tanizaki didn't like to eat alone. When he went out, he'd drag along everyone who happened to be present. (8/80)

MATSUKO: Tanizaki drank mostly sake. He also liked grape-based drinks, especially brandy; he liked wine, too, but didn't drink it often because it made his legs wobbly. He didn't care much for whisky. (7/10/78)

MATSUKO: Tanizaki's favorite sake was Goshun (呉春), made by Nishida Hideo (西田秀生), of Ikeda City, Osaka. Nishida loved Tanizaki's writings so much that in 1945–46, when rice was hard to come by, he carried as much rice as he could to Tanizaki's house in Kyoto, announced that he was a great fan of Tanizaki's writing (先生の愛読者です！) and left the rice at the entrance, without even asking if he could meet the writer. (7/4/77)

MATSUKO: Tanizaki also had a sweet tooth: "If you like sake, you also like sweets," Mrs. Tanizaki said. (7/4/77)

MATSUKO: Tanizaki stopped smoking abruptly at the age of forty or forty-one and never smoked again. Mrs. Tanizaki said she was very impressed with his ability to stop abruptly. (7/4/77)

Pastimes

MATSUKO: Tanizaki played word games with Emiko—they had their own language, with words for people and things. (8/20/72)

MATSUKO: He invented a language that only members of the family could understand. He had little communication with Ayuko or with his siblings—he was concerned about them, but was not at ease with them. Even with Emiko, he was ill at ease unless they spoke in their special language, and then his conversation was half-joking (冗談半分). (7/4/77)

MATSUKO: In late years, Tanizaki didn't read much at night because his eyes had grown weak. What did he enjoy reading? His own early works, and English translations of his novels. (7/4/77)

TAKEDA AYUKO: Tanizaki liked Pearl Buck's work and went to see a movie version of *The Good Earth*. (7/12/77)

Both Mrs. Tanizaki and Shūhei said that Tanizaki liked American movies. He enjoyed Chaplin.

SHŪHEI: Jun'ichirō liked cheerful, optimistic movies, not psychological treatments. He liked Hitchcock; in Japan, he liked Ozu best, then Mizoguchi. (7/12/77)

MATSUKO: Though Tanizaki was always fond of movies, he preferred radio to television. He'd go to sleep with the radio on; if someone turned it off, he'd wake up. (8/5/79)

MATSUKO: Tanizaki's hobbies included writing, eating, movies, kabuki, music, and calligraphy. He had no unwholesome pastimes, like racing. Moving was another hobby. (8/5/79)

What did Tanizaki like to talk about?

MATSUKO: He wouldn't discuss literature at relaxed times. He'd talk about it with professionals, but couldn't stand to listen to amateurs go on about literature (絶対文学の話はしませんでした。玄人ならいいが素人の文学話は我慢できない). He enjoyed talking about movies and theater, and was very alert (非常に敏感) for new developments in the news. He was clumsy with machines but fascinated with them anyway. (7/4/77)

What kind of music did Tanizaki like?

MATSUKO: In Western music, piano. He was interested in *kamigata jiuta* and practiced the shamisen. (4/19/71)

MATSUKO: Around 1930 Tanizaki was particularly enthusiastic (熱心) about *jiuta*. In Western music, he loved Wagner. Once when a Wagner opera was performed in Tokyo, he insisted on going, even though he was suffering from angina at the time. Mrs. Tanizaki herself favored Chopin. (7/4/77)

MATSUKO: In his late years Tanizaki bought cars—first a Toyota, then a sturdy European car (Mrs. Tanizaki doesn't remember the make, but it wasn't a Benz or Volvo), and had a live-in driver. Mrs. Tanizaki's first husband, a great car fancier, had Cadillacs and Packards in the 'twenties. (8/5/79)

TANIZAKI'S WORKS

Mrs. Tanizaki's own impression of Tanizaki's writings: "I can relax and read them without feeling any anxiety whatever" (安心しきって読める). (1/12/83)

TAKEDA AYUKO, TANIZAKI SHŪHEI, MATSUKO: Tanizaki liked craftsmanship and technical skill (技巧) in fiction, especially in his early years. He disliked sentimentalism in any form—in films, novels, or real life. But the definition of sentimentalism was a problem: Ayuko, Matsuko, and Shūhei denied that kabuki is sentimental; *melodrama* (the English word) is sentimental, Shūhei said. (7/12/77)

YAMAGUCHI KŌICHI: Tanizaki never talked about works he was writing or thinking about. He let the ideas smolder inside himself. (4/19/78)

MATSUKO: He didn't want anyone to read his manuscripts before publication or during writing, because someone might say "Please don't write this" (これを書かないでください), causing him to lose his freedom and be unable to write. (4/18/80)

YAMAGUCHI MITSUKO: Tanizaki was always immersed in what he was writing—he only emerged for meals and tea, and never engaged in small talk. (8/80)

MATSUKO: After Tanizaki's death, several books he had ordered arrived from the bookseller, including Dōgen's *Shōbōgenzō* [道元, 『正法眼蔵』, "Treasury of the True Dharma Eye," 13th century] and Sartre on existentialism—books he was going to refer to in writing his next work? (7/4/77)

Sorrows of a Heretic (『異端者の悲しみ』 , 1917)

TANIZAKI SHŪHEI: It presents a fairly accurate picture of the family, but Tanizaki made some distortions for the sake of humor (滑稽), which he used to avoid sentimentalism. (7/12/77)

The Plays

YAMAGUCHI KŌICHI: *Okuni and Gohei* (『お国と五平』 , 1922) resembles European drama. It's short (one hour) and has only three characters. Tanizaki's masterpiece, it will endure. But Tanizaki wasn't really a dramatist; he was an amateur. The structure (くみたて) is simplistic.

The Tale of Hōjōji (『法成寺物語』 , 1915), a play on a large scale, has the freshness of an amateur; it introduced a new pattern.

Yamaguchi dislikes *The Age of Terror* (『恐怖時代』 , 1916). (8/13/77)

KATAOKA NIZAEMON XIII: Some say that Tanizaki's plays are difficult for actors because there's so much dialogue, but Nizaemon says that the lines, though long, are easy to memorize because they're logical (台詞が多くてもちゃんと理屈が通っているから覚えやすい). They're written carefully (言葉が丁寧に書いてある).

When Tanizaki's plays are produced, are they cut or revised? Nizaemon performs them as written (そのまま). Since Tanizaki put so much care into his dialogue, it would be wrong (わるい) to make changes.

Is Tanizaki's dialogue good as kabuki? Yes, very good—better than that of other modern authors who've written for kabuki. Nizaemon's companion said that the content of Tanizaki's plays was difficult, but Nizaemon disagreed. Kabuki would grow (発展) if there were more playwrights like Tanizaki, he said.

Nizaemon's favorite Tanizaki plays? *The Murder of Otsuya* [『お艶殺し』, 1915; translated as "A Springtime Case;" a novella adapted to the stage], especially the role of Serizawa, which is profound (おくぶかい) and fun to perform (楽しみがあった). He also likes *Because I Love Her* (『愛すればこそ』, 1921–22), *The Loveless Ones* (『愛なき人々』, 1923), and *The Tale of Hōjōji*. Also: Funahashi Seiichi's dramatization of *Captain Shigemoto's Mother* (『少将滋幹の母』, 1949), in which Mitsugorō was superb (すばらしかった) as Kunitsune.

Tanizaki didn't much want to watch his own plays (自分の作った物を余り見たくない), but he did come to see *The Murder of Otsuya*. (7/15/77)

Naomi (痴人の愛, 1925)

I told Mrs. Tanizaki that I'd seen the new film version (*Naomi*, 1980, directed by Takabayashi Yōichi). She said it had been well reviewed and that she'd heard the woman's nude scenes were especially good! The novel sells well, she said, and even young people (such as her granddaughter Kanze Akome) find it exciting reading. (4/18/80)

Choosing a Cover Illustration for My Translation of Naomi

[Knopf found a painting by Takehisa Yumeji (竹久夢二, 1884–1934) that they wanted to use on the cover, but the owner of the painting refused to give permission. Mrs. Tanizaki interceded at my request, but even she was unable to persuade the owner. In the summer of 1985, she and I met at International House, in Tokyo, to discuss alternatives.] She arrived late in the afternoon with a Miss Uchida, whose father is a curator at the Suntory Museum, bearing several Yumeji books and ready to recommend a specific painting. By coincidence, they had selected the *same painting* that Knopf had favored and whose owner had said "no." None of the other Yumeji prints or paintings seemed as suitable as that one, and so Mrs. Tanizaki is going to consult with a Mr. Komatsu at the National Museum about what to do next.

One of the Yumeji pictures we looked at, "Black Cat" (黒猫), depicts a brown-haired woman with round, blue eyes and a pink blouse, holding a black cat. Mrs. Tanizaki said the woman in the painting looks like O-Sei, Tanizaki's sister-in-law [Seiko, Chiyo's younger sister and the inspiration for Naomi]. It might be good on a cover for *A Cat, a Man, and Two Women* (『猫と圧造と二人のをんな』, 1936). Seiko also looked like Marlene Dietrich, Mrs. Tanizaki said. (7/2/85) [Ultimately, Knopf was able to convince the owner of everyone's first choice to allow its use on the cover of the first edition of my translation.]

Tanizaki Shūhei told me that he'd gone to the Maruzen bookstore at Tokyo Station to buy a copy of my translation of *The Secret History of the Lord of Musashi and Arrowroot*. When I offered to send him a copy of my *Naomi* translation, he declined. "I know the model," he snapped, by way of explanation. [He was referring to O-Sei.] (summer 1985)

Arrowroot (『吉野葛』, 1931)

MATSUKO: Tanizaki intended to write about "the Heavenly King" (Jitennō 自天王) when he began planning *Arrowroot*—he had gathered all the sources and materials for it, but, as he says in the story, he changed his mind. Mrs. Tanizaki thinks the reason was political. Jitennō is still revered in the mountains of Yoshino— there's a festival for him, and people feel strongly about their history. A novel on Jitennō would inevitably reflect these sentiments; but as a figure of the Southern Court, Jitennō is *persona non grata* to adherents of the victorious Northern Court, and so in 1930 it would have been awkward to write sympathetically about him. (6/22/73)

ONOE ROKUJIRŌ: In 1925 or 1926 Tanizaki's sister Sueko had been hospitalized in Kyoto. As it happens, Rokujirō's mother was in the next room. Rokusaburō, Rokujirō's father, got acquainted with Tanizaki at the hospital.

In October 1930 Tanizaki arrived at the Sakura Kadan Inn, in Yoshino, with six large trunks, containing books, clothing, and a shamisen. As he settled down to dinner, he asked the maids if they knew a soy-sauce maker named Onoe. They explained the relationship between the inn and the Onoe family: the innkeeper, Tatsumi Chōraku, was Rokujirō's father-in-law. Tanizaki telephoned immediately and invited the Onoes to come see him. Rokujirō went the next day with his father. The weather was cold and, since there were few other guests, Tanizaki could use as many hibachi as he wanted; they were placed all over the room. Tanizaki was wearing a brown, sleeveless jacket (そでなし). At the time, Rokujirō was a twenty-six-year-old, self-styled "literary youth" (文学青年). (8/9–10/77)

At Yoshino I was able to stay at the Sakura Kadan—in fact, in the same room that Tanizaki and the Shōwa emperor had stayed in. Tanizaki's maid at the inn at the time, Dogura Setsuko (土倉せつ子), runs a souvenir shop next door. She was quite willing to talk. Tanizaki was heavy-set, she said, cut a fine figure (りっぱ), and looked older than he was [forty-four]. Though he had brought a lot of luggage, he kept the room neat. He always wore a kimono; he sat in his room, beside the hibachi, writing all day; he rarely called for her and hardly talked with her at all; he played the shamisen when he was tired or bored; he liked meat—sukiyaki—but didn't eat or drink excessively; and he went outside only with Onoe Rokujirō. (My diary, 6/26/77)

According to Rokujirō, Setsuko said to Tanizaki, "You must be lonely in a remote place like this" (先生はこんなところへ来て寂しいやろう). Tanizaki replied, "No one is waiting for me at home. There's only the cat." (いいえ、家でも誰も待っていない。猫だけしかいない). (8/9–10/77)

Meals were something of a problem at the inn, said Rokujirō, because there was little variety in the Yoshino diet, and an inn could hardly serve the same meals over and over to a long-term guest. They explained the situation to Tanizaki, adding that there was plenty of beef, but not much else. Very fond of beef, Tanizaki was delighted. (8/9–10/77)

Rokujirō said he took Tanizaki to his house, and together they walked around Kamiichi. Tanizaki wore *hakama* and *haori* over his kimono, and clogs on his feet, and always carried a notebook in the breast of his kimono. The fried rice-cakes (餅) made by a Kamiichi shop called Kobashi delighted him. Onoe commented, "That's about the only good thing there is to eat in Yoshino" (吉野で美味しいものはそれぐらいだから). Tanizaki also enjoyed the unusual sight of water being drawn up directly from the Yoshino River into the houses along the banks.

Tanizaki wanted to watch the process of paper being made by hand, and so Rokujirō, Chōraku, and Tanizaki walked together from Onoe's house to Miyataki and Natsumi. Rokujirō carried the lunch boxes. They had telephoned ahead and were expected. At Natsumi they were shown the Hatsune drum; Tanizaki took notes. Ripe persimmons (じゅくし) were served. Tanizaki was given *five* of them to take with him; being large and filling, they would last him for days. Rokujirō was given the task of carrying them all the way to Kuzu (by bus), where they watched paper being made, and then back to the inn. The persimmons had to be carried flat and with great care lest they get squashed. (8/9–10/77)

Rokujirō, too, is convinced that Tanizaki went to Yoshino with the intention of writing an historical novel instead of *Arrowroot*. "I'm positive" (断言できます), he said. Why? Because Tanizaki asked Chōraku, who was extremely knowledgeable, to tell him about the history of the Southern Court; and he asked Rokujirō to guide him to sites associated with the Court, such as Sannokō, where Jitennō hid, and which is difficult of access even today. Tanizaki never discussed what he was working on, but Rokujirō got the impression that he wanted to write about Jitennō and the Southern Court. (8/9–10/77)

The Makioka Sisters (『細雪』, 1943–48)

MATSUKO: Tanizaki's own favorite—the one he considered his best work—was *The Makioka Sisters*. He referred to it as his masterpiece. (4/19/71)

When did he begin *The Makioka Sisters*? Mrs. Tanizaki says she's not good at dates, but she says he planned (腹案) the novel while working on his first *Genji* translation [begun in 1935] and started writing it after finishing *A Cat, a Man, and Two Women* [1937]. (7/4/77)

MATSUKO: Planning (構想) was long and painful, and "he was grumpy until he started writing; but once he began to write, he'd brighten up and start telling jokes. The jokes were all plays on words" (書き出すまで機嫌が悪いけれども書き出したら明るくなって冗談を言い出します。冗談はみんな言葉の遊びでございまして). (7/4/77)

MATSUKO: During the war, as he was writing *The Makioka Sisters*, was he confident that the war would end soon and he'd be able to publish it? No, toward the end of the war he was pessimistic (悲観的). At Katsuyama, where they had gone to escape the American bombing of major cities, he had very little money left and spoke of becoming an English or Japanese teacher at some middle school: in that era there was nothing else he could have done; there was no market for a writer like him. The end of the war came as a great relief to him (ほっとしたのは本当の気持ち). (7/4/77)

MATSUKO: Tanizaki had Mrs. Tanizaki correct the dialect in the dialogue of *The Makioka Sisters*, but she hesitated to change very much—he was, after all, the master of style. But now, as she rereads it, she finds expressions that are slightly unnatural and wishes she had revised them. (8/4/77)

I asked about the poems in *The Makioka Sisters*. She composed all of them herself, Mrs. Tanizaki said. Tanizaki made a few changes here and there, but all the poems are hers, including (I asked specifically) いとせめて花見衣に . . . , at the end of I:19. She seemed pleased to be asked. I think she's proud of her poetry; and she said everyone assumed that all the poems in the novel had been written by Tanizaki. (12/30/86)

Is *The Makioka Sisters* an accurate picture of the Tanizaki household at the time?

MATSUKO: Yes. An example is the bee incident [I:20]. When she read the novel, she thought, "When did he write that down?" She also mentioned the scenes of a lady using her compact on the train [I:11], and the Makiokas dining with their Russian friends [I:17]. She doubled up laughing as she recalled passing the food they couldn't eat to the dog under the table. (7/4/77)

MATSUKO: The dinner with the Russians really happened, and it was largely as described in the novel. Their name was Simonoff [シモ ノフ]; someone named Vronsky was present, as well. Tanizaki had read *Anna Karenina* and went with Mrs. Tanizaki to see a film adaptation [probably the 1935 version starring Greta Garbo and Frederic March]. (7/10/78)

Mrs. Tanizaki praised the commentary (解説) Tanabe Seiko wrote for the new, one-volume Chūkō Bunko edition of *The Makioka Sisters*. She said that she particularly agreed with the connection Tanabe draws between the world of the novel and the era of the Heian court. She and Tanizaki both, from their youth, were drawn to the Heian period, to what Tanabe calls "a culture of women" (女文化), in preference to the male-, samurai-dominated periods that followed. It's a taste they shared, a mutual affinity. She emphasized it strongly, but had trouble pinning down exactly what it was about the Heian period that appealed to them—a sensitivity to beauty? elegance? (1/12/83)

YAMAGUCHI KŌICHI: Tanizaki liked the artist Suga Tatehiko [菅楯 彦, 1978–1963], a second-rate painter (says Yamaguchi), when no one else did, and praised him extravagantly, not caring what anyone else said about him. He had Suga do the cover and illustrations for some of his works, including *The Makioka Sisters*. When Tanizaki heard that Suga had died, the first thing he said was that it was a shame to lose such a handsome man (好男子). Tanizaki tried to see character through a person's face, and was very perceptive. He looked for what was behind the beauty—culture, refinement, education. (4/19/78)

A Record of Cruelty (『残虐記』, 1958)

I asked Mrs. Tanizaki why Tanizaki left *A Record of Cruelty* unfinished. Ibuki Kazuko wonders if pressure from Hiroshima survivors had something to do with it. Not that she remembers, Mrs. Tanizaki replied. His health wasn't good at the time, and probably he was no longer in a mood to continue with it (気分が乗らなくなってしまった). (8/17/85)

Seven Japanese Tales

HOWARD HIBBETT: Tanizaki, Harold Strauss, and Hibbett selected the contents of *Seven Japanese Tales*. Tanizaki specifically wanted to include "The Thief" [「私」, 1921] and "The Little Kingdom" [「小さな大國」, 1918]. Hibbett vetoed the latter; Strauss insisted on including "The Tattooer" [「刺青」, 1910]. Tanizaki was glad to have "A Portrait of Shunkin," "The Bridge of Dreams" [「夢の浮き橋」, 1959], and "A Blind Man's Tale" [「盲目物語」, 1932] included, as well. (5/6/77) ["The Little Kingdom" was later translated by Paul McCarthy.]

HAROLD STRAUSS: "I know that it appears in our book, SEVEN

JAPANESE TALES, as Shisei, but Tanizaki himself, shortly before his death, told me that it should be read Irezumi." (Letter to me, 1/19/72)

THE NOBEL PRIZE

MATSUKO: If Japan's turn had come sooner, Tanizaki would have received the Nobel Prize, Mrs. Tanizaki said confidently. Tanizaki's attitude about rumors that he would receive the prize: "The honor would be of no consequence" (名誉はどうでもいい), but "I could use the money" (お金は助かります). He also worried about the demands on his time that would follow from winning the Prize—press conferences, and so on. Poor Mr. Kawabata wasn't able to get any work done after he won the prize, she said. [The rumors that Tanizaki was a candidate for the prize were confirmed many years later.] (7/4/77)

CRITICS

Paul McCarthy asked who among Japanese critics had a deep understanding of and sympathy for Tanizaki's works. No one, Mrs. Tanizaki said. Americans, particularly Howard Hibbett, seem to understand his writings better than contemporary Japanese. (7/4/77)

COMMENTS ON THEATER

Tanizaki said that kabuki plays are foolish and vulgar (馬鹿、下品), according to Shūhei. He went to see the actors, not the plays. (7/12/77)

Yamaguchi Kōichi disagreed emphatically with Shūhei. Many Japanese prefer the actors over the plays, he said, including writers; but never Tanizaki. He did have his favorite actors, but he liked kabuki for itself. Far from Tanizaki pursuing actors, actors pursued him. His favorite was Kikugorō VI. (8/13/77)

MATSUKO: When he was on his deathbed and all the family members were gathered around weeping and wailing, Kikugorō said crossly, "Not so fast!" (まだはやいよ). Tanizaki wasn't present, but heard about it from people who were there. (8/5/79)

MATSUKO: Tanizaki liked Sawamura Tosshō V [1933–2001; later took the name Sawamura Sōjūrō IX], predicted that he'd be a great actor. (8/20/72)

Mrs. Tanizaki insisted that Tanizaki was interested in the Bunraku puppet theater even late in his life; Shūhei had the impression that Tanizaki had lost interest; they compromised by agreeing that he was still interested, but less so than in the late 1920s. Mrs. Tanizaki added that in late years Tanizaki like the storytellers (*yose, rakugo*) best; Shūhei agreed; traditional storytelling held a nostalgic attraction for him. "Because television is boring" (つまらない), added Shūhei. Ayuko put in that Tanizaki had enjoyed magic shows when she was a little girl. (7/12/77)

HIGUCHI TOMIMARO: Tanizaki enjoyed the storytellers (落語) of Western Japan, which was unusual for a Tokyo man. He used to go hear them frequently in Kyoto right after the war, thinking it would be a good way to learn the dialect. (7/27/77)

Matsuko is very familiar with the kabuki world. She knows the actors and their families and the gossip about them. Her favorite is Tamasaburō [五代目坂東玉三郎, b. 1950]—she talks about him all the time, has books by and about him, and has a large color picture of him on the wall, along with an engaging, but much smaller, photo of a smiling Tanizaki. (8/5/79)

MATSUKO: Tamasaburō possesses an eroticism (色気) above and beyond the old-time onnagata. Kankurō [1955–2012, grandson of Kikugorō VI and son of Kanzaburō XVII] will be a great actor, she said. Kikugorō VI was truly great. (8/20/72) [She was right: Kankurō went on to become Kanzaburō XVIII and was one of the most celebrated kabuki actors of his generation.]

MATSUKO: Tamasaburō is exactly the image Tanizaki had in mind for Otsuya, and Mrs. Tanizaki wishes Tanizaki could have seen Tamasaburō in that role. She's a great fan of Tamasaburō's, especially in his "evil woman" roles. (7/4/77)

I took Mrs. Tanizaki and Tamasaburō to dinner at Taimeiken, in Nihonbashi, which is run by an acquaintance of mine. We were given a private room. Mrs. Tanizaki and Tamasaburō had met before, but had never had a chance to talk. Their rapport as they spoke of art, death, and other subjects was astonishing. She says she has some secrets about the kabuki world that she learned from Tanizaki and wants to pass on to Tamasaburō, but she'll wait until I get to Japan again and bring us together. She said she never talked even with Tanizaki in such depth as with Tamasaburō that evening. (8/11/79)

Tamasaburō said he loves and admires women who, like Mrs. Tanizaki, have overcome the grief and loneliness of being left behind and attained a state (境地) of serenity. Mrs. Tanizaki was silent for a moment, then said softly, and with a quizzical look, "I wonder if I'll ever reach that state." (8/11/79)

As for Tanizaki's famous waywardness (わがまま): Everyone feels that way, said Tamasaburō to Mrs. Tanizaki, but most people hide it. (8/11/79)

Mrs. Tanizaki asked if I thought Americans got much out of kabuki when it was performed in New York. I said I thought (from what I'd overheard in the lobby and read in reviews) that even viewers who don't know much about kabuki could pick out the good actors—Kanzaburō XVII, Tamasaburō, Tomijūrō [五代目中村富十郎, 1929–2011]—without knowing their reputations. Free from biases, Americans have a fresh perspective on kabuki, I said.

She said that Tamasaburō has grown increasingly selfish and wayward recently. He has moved out of his mother's house and has his own "mansion" (condo) now. She doesn't often go to kabuki any more; "it's so long," she says. (8/17/85)

MATSUKO: A story about Hanayagi Shōtarō [花柳章太郎, 1894–1965] and Mizutani Yaeko [水谷八重子, 1905–1979]: They starred together in a stage version of *Diary of a Mad Old Man*, with Hanayagi as the old man and Yaeko as Satsuko. (Tanizaki insisted on casting Yaeko, though she protested that she was too old for the role.) Later, Hanayagi sent to Tanizaki the ink footprints he had made of Yaeko's feet during the production. Tanizaki was embarrassed (こまった、こまった). Hanayagi was an old friend of Mrs. Tanizaki's—they corresponded for years; he always illustrated his letters with skillful drawings. (2/22/80)

I met Mrs. Tanizaki and Emiko at the Suidobashi Hōshō Noh Theater. Emiko looks unmistakably like Mrs. Tanizaki but is heavier. We saw Kanze Hideo [観世栄夫, Emiko's husband, 1927–2007] perform *Yorimasa*. Later I told Mrs. Tanizaki I'd seen him play a tough detective on television. She laughed and said that his children had been embarrassed by his playing that role. "Don't do it" (やめてくれ), they said—he was too old-fashioned for such parts, and the other children laughed at them in school. (4/18/80)

Mrs. Tanizaki laments the fact that Tamasaburō doesn't enjoy fine dining, as she does. Recently she had a long telephone conversation with him. She started by saying, "Let me voice some complaints" (悪口を言わせてください). She grumbled about actors whom she couldn't visit backstage, blasting Kankurō, Kichiemon [二代目中村吉右衛門, b. 1944], and Somegorō [六代目染五郎, later Kōshirō IX 九代目松本幸四郎, b. 1942], in particular. She praised Takao [片岡孝夫, who became Nizaemon XV, b. 1944], but added that it's sad Takao is considered outstanding—it just shows how bad the situation has become—and Tomijūrō. To Tamasaburō, apparently, she also blasted Utaemon [六代目中村歌右衛門, 1917–2001]. How did Tamasaburō's Okaru (in *Chūshingura*) compare to other actors', I asked? Far superior, she said forcefully. (4/18/80)

COMMENTS ON OTHER WRITERS

Fyodor Dostoyevsky (1821-1881)

MATSUKO: Tanizaki read Dostoyevsky, whose work he preferred over Tolstoy's, and often talked about him and his [first] wife. (7/10/78)

Shimazaki Tōson (島崎藤村, 1872-1943)

MATSUKO: Regarding Tōson's *Before the Dawn* [『夜明け前』, 1929–1935], Tanizaki said, "I'm not impressed; it doesn't appeal to me" (感心しない、ぴんとこない). He didn't care for Tōson's work in general. (7/4/77)

What did Tanizaki think about writing of his family, as in *The Makioka Sisters*, as Tōson did?

MATSUKO: Tanizaki detested Tōson and said a writer shouldn't jeopardize his relatives the way Tōson had; Tanizaki avoided writing anything damaging about his family. (4/18/80)

Izumi Kyōka (泉鏡花,1973-1939)

Mrs. Tanizaki said that Kyōka was rigid, with an inflexible schedule and inflexible rules for his house. He "suffered from an obsession with cleanliness" (爛症病み). For example, one was expected to undress before going to the toilet, because the odor would penetrate one's clothes. She recommended a book by Kyōka's niece Natsuki (名月), which describes the same rules applied by Kyōka's widow when Natsuki lived with her in Atami. Mrs. Tanizaki remembers seeing Natsuki in those days and wondering why she was so thin and frail. Now she knows that it was because Kyōka's widow wouldn't give her enough to eat. (7/27/79) Nevertheless, Tanizaki respected Kyōka so much that he asked Kyōka to serve as go-between for Ayuko's marriage. (7/4/77)

Nagai Kafū (永井荷風, 1879-1959)

MATSUKO: Tanizaki had great respect for Kafū, but was not comfortable with him—Tanizaki was awkwardly shy (てれや) with people who praised him, as Kafū did, and even toward his family. (7/4/77)

Kawabata Yasunari (川端康成, 1899-1972)

MATSUKO: Kawabata had piercing eyes—as if he could size up a person completely at a glance. (8/20/72)

Seidensticker said that Kawabata was very much like his work—"delicate astringency," at first view a formidable man. Warm and friendly, but there was a streak of coldness, even cruelty. (1989)

Shiga Naoya (志賀直哉, 1883-1971)

MATSUKO: Tanizaki asked Shiga, who had just returned from Europe, what appealed to him about traveling there. Shiga replied that, by traveling, "one comes to know what's good about Japan" (日本の良さが分かる). (7/27/79)

I met Mrs. Tanizaki at the Kanzes' and went to dinner with her and her son, Watanabe Seiji, at Fuku Sushi, where Mishima and his disciple Morita ate their last dinner together. Mrs. Tanizaki had come from an afternoon with Shiga Naoya's widow. She said she stayed longer than she had planned (and so was late meeting us) because Mrs. Shiga wept and wouldn't let her leave. Fuku Sushi offers an exaggeratedly macho atmosphere—the chefs' shouts of *irasshai!!!* were deafening—except in the rest room, which was decorated as I imagine a 19th-century French brothel might have been. (7/29/75)

I told Mrs. Tanizaki that I'd just read Shiga's *A Dark Night's Passing* [暗夜行路, 1921–1937]. She was surprisingly open in her comments about the novel and about Shiga. He had no imagination, she said, and that's why he wrote only about himself. (5/11/80)

Mishima Yukio (三島由紀夫, 1925-1970), Natsume Sōseki (夏目
漱石, 1867-1916), Mori Ōgai (森鷗外, 1862-1922),
and Kōda Rohan (幸田露伴, 1867–1947)

MATSUKO: Tanizaki praised Mishima, thought him the best of the
young writers. He respected (尊敬) Sōseki but didn't really *like*
his works. He felt more affinity with Ōgai and Rohan. (6/22/73)

When I asked what Tanizaki said about Ōgai, Mrs. Tanizaki replied
that once, when she asked him for something to read, he gave her a
first edition of Ōgai's translation of Andersen's *Improvisatoren* [『即
興詩人』, 1902], which they both enjoyed. She heard that much of
the pleasure in it derived from Ōgai's style, which improved the work
over the original. (1/12/83)

MATSUKO: Tanizaki hardly ever read other modern Japanese
writers—"almost never" (ほとんど), she said emphatically. But
he read everything of Mishima's and praised him. He especially liked Mishima's "Beautiful Star" [『美しい星』, 1962] and
wrote Mishima to tell him so. (7/4/77)
MATSUKO: Mishima, in a farewell letter (遺書) to his mentor Shimizu
Fumio [清水文雄, 1903–1998], acknowledged that no other writer, including himself, reached the level of Tanizaki (谷崎に及ぶ
作家は居ない), though he had hesitated to say so before because of his close relationship with Kawabata. (6/22/73)

Seidensticker said that Mishima laughed too much—did he want
to fill silences? There was something phony about him—he always
seemed to be playacting. He was also very interesting and could be
amusing. He mimicked an "education mama" (教育ママ) lecturing
on the moral edification to be gained from reading the works of

Mishima. His "Shield Society" (盾の会) was "a funny little gang of chocolate soldiers." (1989)

Nagai Tatsuo (永井龍男, 1904–1990) and Novels by Maruya Saiichi (丸谷才一, 1925–2012)

Mrs. Tanizaki recommended the short stories of Nagai Tatsuo and two books by Maruya Saiichi, *Singular Rebellion* [『たった一人の反乱』, which won the Tanizaki Prize in 1972] and *Cloistered Emperor Gotoba* [『後鳥羽院』, 1973]. (7/29/73)

Jean-Paul Sartre (1905–1980)

MATSUKO: When Sartre visited Japan in 1967 he told reporters at the airport that the person he had most wanted to meet in Japan was Tanizaki. He went to Yugawara to see Mrs. Tanizaki, but she was in Kyoto at the time. He contacted her and went with her and Simone de Beauvoir to Tanizaki's grave at Hōnen'in. He liked *The Makioka Sisters*, which he had read in English, along with some short stories in French. Mrs. Tanizaki's impression of Sartre: "a very perceptive person" (勘のいいかた); he often understood what she was saying even before the interpreter had finished translating. (7/4/77, 7/2/85)

Yosano Akiko (与謝野晶子, 1878–1942)

Mrs. Tanizaki singled out Akiko as a free, modern woman for whom she has great respect. (1/12/83)

Uno Chiyo (宇野千代, 1897–1996)

When I asked which women writers today stand out, Mrs. Tanizaki replied that no one in particular came to mind. After further thought, she mentioned Uno Chiyo as someone "big" (大きい) . She mentioned *Ohan* [おはん, 1947], when asked to recommend a work by Uno. (1/15/88)

Tawara Machi (俵万智, b. 1962)

On Chiba Shunji's recommendation, I bought Tawara Machi's collection of poems *Salad Anniversary* [サラダ記念日, 1987]. I asked Mrs. Tanizaki about it. She and the others praised it. Very immediate—sharp images. It's wonderful that young people are reading poetry. Might it lead to a revival [of waka]? (1/12/83)

On the literary scene today in general? It's "a contest among acorns," that is, there's not much to choose from (ドングリの背比べ), Mrs. Tanizaki said. (1/12/83)

TANIZAKI MATSUKO

Mrs. Tanizaki's first impressions of Tokyo, in the spring of 1923: Tokyo was greener than Osaka (that is, it had more trees and other vegetation); the palace moat was beautiful; Tokyo people were cold. She saw the premier of Tanizaki's play *White Fox Hot Spring* [『白狐の湯』, 1923] at the Teikoku Gekijo [Imperial Theater]. (8/5/79)

MATSUKO: Mrs. Tanizaki's oldest sister continued to speak Osaka dialect even in Tokyo. In the old days Mrs. Tanizaki was embarrassed to ride with her on the train in Tokyo, because of the stares they received, but people don't pay attention any more. This is probably the effect of television broadcasts in the Osaka and Kyoto dialects. (8/20/72)

At lunch with Mrs. Tanizaki and Watanabe Shigeko: Mrs. Watanabe was very talkative (for her) and friendly. She and Mrs. Tanizaki often say exactly the same thing at once; realizing it, Mrs. Watanabe stops and lets Mrs. Tanizaki finish. (7/29/73)

Mrs. Tanizaki abruptly changed the subject after lunch and, looking down, mumbled that she had made great sacrifices for Tanizaki's work. After Tanizaki died, Shiga Naoya said to her that, even conceding "art for art's sake," he wouldn't have been able to do what Tanizaki did [i.e., urge Mrs. Tanizaki to abort their child in 1938] (いくら芸術至上と言っても、主人がしたようなことは出来ません). At the time, Shimanaka [head of Chūō Kōron] told her that she should have the child, no matter what Tanizaki said. She wishes she had followed his advice; the child would be in his thirties now. To make it worse, Tanizaki himself, when he got older and less inflexible, regretted what he had done (くやみました).

This line of conversation plunged all of us into a few minutes of grim silence. Mrs. Tanizaki broke it by saying that Tanizaki was always polite to the servants, saying "thank you" (ありがとう) as each plate was brought to the table. (7/4/77)

As an example of how painful it could be to live with Tanizaki, Mrs. Tanizaki mentioned (at dinner with Tamasaburō) her shock upon reading Tanizaki's poem "No one knows my heart but me" (我といふ人の心はだだひとり我よりほかに知る人はなし). (8/11/79)

MATSUKO: Some good places to visit in Kyoto: Kōdaiji (高台寺); Kobori Enshū's (小堀遠州) house, in Kohōan (孤篷庵), at

Daitokuji (大徳寺); Shinjuan (真珠庵) and Jukōin (聚光院), the temple that contains Rikyū's (利休) grave, both in Daitokuji; Kōetsuji (光悦寺); Shisendō (詩仙堂); Jōjakkōji (常寂光寺), a good place for cherry blossoms; Kōzanji (高山寺). (4/19/71) Favorite places near Kyoto to go in the summer: the Hieizan Hotel, for the view; the boats and islands of Lake Biwa; the Uji Bridge (memories of *Genji*); Ishiyamadera [where, according to legend, Murasaki Shikibu wrote *The Tale of Genji*]. (8/17/86)

Mrs. Tanizaki is amused and puzzled by young peoples' fashions. She chuckled at some young people in the coffee shop and whispered to me, "What do you think of these fashions?" (8/20/72)

What musical instruments do you (Mrs. Tanizaki) play? Koto and shamisen; used to play the piano, especially Chopin. (4/19/71)

Mrs. Tanizaki likes cotton candy. (8/20/72)

Mrs. Tanizaki has a collection of dolls and toys from around the world, reflecting what she calls her "little-girl's taste" (少女趣味). (8/5/79)

She thinks that the Japanese people are essentially cheerful (あかるい), rarely gloomy (陰気). (12/29/82)

Mrs. Tanizaki said that she advised her daughter, Emiko, not to marry an artist, because it's mentally exhausting (気苦労が多いから芸術家と結婚しないように), and asked friends to search for a salaryman for her to marry. She had more than thirty marriage-meetings (見合い)—"It was *The Makioka Sisters* all over again" (『細雪』の繰り返し). Emiko was turned down by some, she herself turned down more. Being used to the Tanizaki household, she found the conversation of ordinary people boring—there was nothing to talk about—and so she was not easily satisfied. Finally, at the age of twenty-eight, she married the Noh actor Kanze Hideo. (7/4/77)

MATSUKO: Shortly after Tanizaki's death, a robber broke into the Yugawara house while Mrs. Tanizaki and Shigeko slept. The robber cut through the screen and opened the sliding door. Mrs. Tanizaki felt a blast of cold air (it was winter) and thought that Shigeko had opened the door. "It's cold" (寒いじゃないの) she said crossly, and sat up. Standing near her was a man with his face covered except for eye slits, holding a large knife with a foot-long blade, which he held above her threateningly. At first she pulled the quilt over her face; but then she realized that Shigeko was more in danger of being cut that she was, since Shigeko was on the side of the room by the door and veranda, near the man; and the house was full of servants, even her grandchild. She wanted to get rid of the robber as fast as she could, without rousing or endangering the rest of the household. And so, very calmly (she said it's odd how one can be calm and collected at such a time), she said, "I'll give you all the money I have here, but I want you to leave immediately. I promise not to call the police." The robber was concerned about catching the trolley, which would start running in an hour. She promised not to call anyone before then and implored him to leave. He demanded more money. She had some put away, which she gave him, and he left.

When she finally did call the police (after keeping her promise to wait for the trolley to start running), she wanted to avoid publicity and tried to have it reported indirectly by a neighbor. But newsmen at the police station heard of it immediately, and within thirty minutes an NHK [television network] camera-news team was at the house. At the same time, a group of men from Chūō Kōron rushed to the house to deal with the reporters, whom they fended off by saying that Mrs. Tanizaki was resting, trying to recover from the shock, and couldn't talk to anyone. In fact she was giving a statement to the police, who scolded her for not calling sooner; but they were impressed by her composure in the face of the huge blade, which they found in the garden.

The police suggested that she get a house-dog. A dog in the garden can be silenced by a robber, but not one inside. A comparatively odorless breed was recommended, and the result is that the Kanze house is overrun with that breed. Because of the way the dogs tyrannize the house, Mrs. Tanizaki refers to them as "the Honorable Dogs" (お犬様), with a nod to the Tokugawa shogun Tsunayoshi, who required everyone to address dogs politely.

She had an idea who the robber might have been. The police, figuring it was someone who knew his way around the house, questioned all the carpenters and others who might be familiar with the house. She thinks it was a man at the butcher shop who disappeared the same night and wasn't seen again. But she didn't mention him to the police, as he might not have been the one, and she didn't want to cause trouble for an innocent person.

Later in the day, she expressed her concern that Japan might turn into a police state. She didn't like the trend of things—the police had too much power, and at the slightest sign of trouble the riot police (機動隊) were mobilized. (8/5/79)

MATSUKO: In October 1979 her collected essays, written since *Ishōan no yume* [her first memoir, 1967], will be published, she said. Then she can relax and travel a bit; she will have done her best for Tanizaki and can live for herself now. [In fact the collection of essays wasn't published until 1983. A third volume of memoirs was published posthumously in 1998.] (8/5/79)

MATSUKO: In her publications she always refers to herself as Tanizaki's wife (夫人). She hates the word *joshi* (女史) [used to refer to accomplished women] and dislikes "widow" (未亡人). When editors try to identify her as a writer or essayist (随筆家),

she has them delete the label. She brings Tanizaki into everything she writes, even in her articles about kimono. (8/5/79)

Mrs. Tanizaki always had an interest in writing (文学少女). She loved to read (Akutagawa and Arishima Takeo [有島武郎, 1878–1923], for example) and to write; but thinking that Tanizaki wouldn't approve, she hid her writing from him and didn't let on how much she read. Now she's free to write and enjoys it. (1/10/82)

Under Tanizaki's influence, Mrs. Tanizaki, too, has become a gourmet (食いしん坊). She eats well, enjoys eating, and is very particular. (8/5/79)

The other night [4/2/80], on our way to dinner, I urged Mrs. Tanizaki to get in the car first, which is proper; she urged me; it was a standoff, she spluttering, I thinking I was being polite. Her maid saved the day, briskly explaining that, since Mrs. Tanizaki was in kimono, it was easier for her to get in after me. In the cab, I handed her the tea I had brought from China. She clearly wanted to leave it with the maid, who wasn't riding with us, but couldn't get out a request to the driver to wait. Following the maid's example, I briskly asked him to wait a moment. (My diary, 4/5/80)

Taxi to the Okura Hotel for dinner at Yamazato. When we arrived, Mrs. Tanizaki was asked if she had a reservation. No, she said deferentially. But someone recognized her and a table appeared immediately. That's why restaurants often have "reserved" signs on tables. You never know when a Good Person will come in. After dinner she giggled elegantly and said, "It's so much fun to eat good food, isn't it!" (美味しいものをいただくのは楽しいですね!). (4/18/80)

Studios have often made videos of Mrs. Tanizaki so that actresses (in film adaptations of *The Makioka Sisters* and *Shunkin*, for example) can observe her gestures and listen to her speech. (4/18/80)

The poet Minakami Beni commented that "Matsuko-san expresses herself with her hands" (松子さんは手で表現する). This was a keen observation. Her hands are always in motion. (8/28/86)

Mrs. Tanizaki was continually being greeted by friends at the Noh theater. Our seats weren't bad—tenth row, near the center, but one seat was an extra chair placed in the aisle. Mrs. Tanizaki insisted on taking the temporary seat, saying she'd be coming and going a lot, and anyway, she's lighter. She took possession of it while I was in the men's room. We both dozed during the play. I had told her once what Matsui Akira (松井彬, the Noh actor) said about dozing during a Noh performance (it's all right, he said—and a very elegant doze it will be), and she agreed. Most of our dozing occurred during the *aikyōgen* speech. She was wide-awake to watch Hideo when he was on stage. (4/18/80)

Dinner with Mrs. Tanizaki, her granddaughter Akome, Akome's friend Kaoru, and Kaoru's mother, at the Hilton. The pianist played a medley of Christmas carols. Mrs. Tanizaki's eyes grew moist as she listened. Later she told me why: During the occupation, when they were living near Nanzenji, in Kyoto, they became acquainted with an American officer. Passing the house one day, he had heard Emiko playing the piano and stopped to listen, and then asked if he could come inside. He was extremely handsome and gentlemanly. He came again, and again. They went places together, such as to the church near the Heian Shrine. At Christmas they sang carols together. Finally he expressed his desire to marry Emiko. She hesitated, aware of the problems of an international marriage; and as she hesitated, he took it as a "no," or at least not a "yes," and abruptly stopped coming to the house. Fond of him, and sorry to lose touch, they tried to locate him, but were never able to do so. They heard that he'd gone to Korea and thought perhaps he died there, but they never learned. All this came back when she heard the carols. (12/25/81)

I met Mrs. Tanizaki at the Hilton lower lobby. Dinner at Feu 馮, a

French restaurant in Nogizaka. Mrs. Tanizaki looks very well, much better than a year ago. Maybe the "natural vitamins" B and E she's taking.

She says she has an irregular heartbeat (自律神経失調症) [autonomic imbalance, dystonia, says the dictionary], especially at night, but ignores it. (12/29/82)

Mrs. Tanizaki went to hear Seiji Ozawa conduct Beethoven's Ninth at Tange Kenzō's church [the Sekiguchi Catholic Church]—a benefit performance. She was very moved and wished Tanizaki could have heard it. She said it was the sort of thing that makes her grateful to have lived this long. (12/29/82)

At a talk she gave at a women's college, Mrs. Tanizaki was asked if she felt she had changed as a person—or been changed—when she married Tanizaki. Her answer was well received: Tanizaki let her be herself; he lived in such a way that she could develop as herself. One of the professors, less sentimental than the students, said there must have been sad times, as well (悲しいこともあったでしょう). I said the same. She said she'd wept when the professor said what he did; she wept when I said what I did. I believe she thinks mainly of the abortion. (12/29/82)

These days Mrs. Tanizaki talks much less about her husband than she used to—more about herself, her own ideas, kabuki, etc. Tanizaki seems, little by little, to be slipping into the past; we no longer sense his ghost hovering overhead. (1/17/83)

Mrs. Tanizaki was animated as she talked about restrictions on women in pre-Meiji times and the importance of freedom for women. Women can't participate in the culture unless they have some freedom, as they did in the Heian period and since Meiji. Not only that, but when women are not free, the men, too, don't produce the best kind of literature. (1/12/83)

MATSUKO: Women between Heian and Meiji times [i.e., the thirteenth to nineteenth centuries] were like slaves. For one thing (though she's embarrassed to speak of it), there was no sexual freedom. Compare Heian women with the woman in Chikamatsu's play who is destroyed just because she's suspected of adultery.

Tanizaki must have given much thought to the position of women in society, but he died too soon—so much has happened, so much has become clearer since 1965.

The best men's literature from the eras when women were oppressed deals with women's problems—Chikamatsu, for example. (1/17/83)

Mrs. Tanizaki said, "I always want to be beautiful," "I'm always pursuing beauty" (常に美しいものを追求しております). (7/3/85)

An Evening with Mrs. Tanizaki's Fan Club and Other Dinners, 1985

In the evening, still fuzzy with jet lag, I joined Mrs. Tanizaki for dinner with her fan club, the Wakamurasaki no Kai. [The name, which means "The Young Murasaki Club," alludes to chapter 5, "Wakamurasaki" (「若紫」), of *The Tale of Genji* and indirectly to Mrs. Tanizaki, whom Tanizaki compared to the character Murasaki, and whose favorite color was purple (*murasaki*).] Delayed by rain, traffic and the scarcity of cabs, I arrived at the Kanze house late and waited with Emiko for a cab. She kept running up and down the driveway, from the street to the house, poor woman. She has a dear, honest face, plain but loveable.

The dinner was at Muryōan (無量庵), which serves the Ōbaku (黄檗) style of vegetarian *kaiseki*, called *fucha* cuisine (普茶料理), from the Chinese Zen temple Manpukuji (万福寺), in Uji. First Mrs. Tanizaki and I had tea in the tea-room with a fan named Mrs.

Hashimoto. (Mrs. Tanizaki can't drink this tea—it's too strong for her; she had hot water with something floating in it, instead).

The fan club consists of about twenty women of around my age, all wealthy and very presentable. This was their third meeting; they'll meet again in the fall at Fukudaya, at Mrs. Tanizaki's suggestion. I was the only male present. There was constant banter and teasing from the ladies; at times I felt like an employee at a "host club," at times like Terukatsu, in *The Secret History of the Lord of Musashi*: "He felt the eyes of the entire group turn toward him . . . and experienced . . . something like the panic one might feel if surrounded by some exotic tribe. . . . The gathering of women before him was like a flower garden seen for the first time, sparkling with color and redolent of strange incense" (p. 18). (7/3/85)

Mrs. Tanizaki arrived [at International House] by taxi at around 3:30 (having said she'd come after 2:00) with Inazawa Hideo (稲澤秀夫, author of two books on Tanizaki) in tow. They'd been delayed in traffic in Roppongi, and she said she was grateful for Mr. Inazawa's fan. A few minutes after we sat down, the taxi driver rushed in with the fan. Mrs. Tanizaki called out, "Wait, wait" (待ってください、待ってください), as he hurried back toward his car. She pulled a ¥1000 note from her wallet and started to get up, whereupon Inazawa said, "Shall I take it?" She gave it to him, and he took it to the driver. "What a kind driver!" Mrs. Tanizaki said. "Not many would have done that." (7/15/85)

I met Mrs. Tanizaki at the Kanzes'. We went by taxi to the Yamazato restaurant, at the Okura, for dinner. After a week in Karuizawa (which she said was cool and heavenly), she looked older than before, and small and vulnerable. She's hard at work on her autobiography. It will be (if she lives long enough, she says) in five installments to be published by Chūō Kōron in special issues (文芸特集); the first installment, up to elementary school, will appear next month; the second, she says, will be more interesting. She vividly remembers the Meiji

Emperor's death [in 1912]; she was nine. Word reached them in the middle of the night, and her parents wept. How did they get the news, I asked. Radio wasn't widespread yet. Runners with bells at their waists raced through the street, calling out the news, she said. Does she remember General Nogi's suicide, too? Hardly at all; it didn't make much of an impression. The autobiography will go up to her first marriage, in 1923, the year of the earthquake, when she was twenty. We also talked about how hard it is to be in her position, the widow of a great writer. She says she sometimes thinks she should never have published the letters Tanizaki wrote to her, even though everyone tells her she did the right thing, that publication will prevent misunderstandings. After dinner we moved to the spacious and relaxing lobby and asked a hotel man to take several photos of us. She was in no hurry; she was glad to be away from the telephone (and the dogs, I shouldn't wonder). Always running back and forth between her phone and the Kanzes', she gets lots of exercise, she said. (8/17/85)

Dinner with Mrs. Tanizaki at Azusa (梓) in Akasaka, 1986

She looked tired at first, but seemed to get livelier as the evening went on. Typical confusion: she called home to have her maid, Yasuko, get a taxi and come to pick us up, thinking it would be hard to get one at the restaurant. We went out to wait. No Yasuko. I suggested that Mrs. Tanizaki go back inside and sit down. Still no Yasuko. I suggested that we not wait any longer, but take another taxi; there were lots of them. She agreed and left word for Yasuko at the restaurant. When we got to the house, no one was home, and Mrs. Tanizaki couldn't find her key. She insisted that I go on; she'd be fine; the neighbors were relatives and she could wait at their place. But the taxi had left, and I stayed. Then she found her key and went in, finally. (8/13/86)

Mrs. Tanizaki's Birthday Dinner, 1986

To the former Hilton Hotel, now the Capitol Tōkyū, for Mrs.
Tanizaki's birthday dinner, in the same restaurant where she always
dined when it was still the Hilton—the chef and much of the staff
are the same, she says. There were so many guests, I asked Emiko
if there was some special significance to the 83rd birthday. No, she
said; but Mrs. Tanizaki had been ill, and now that she's better she
wanted to have a big party. Almost twenty people were there, including Emiko (her husband was away, performing in Hokkaido), Seiji
[Mrs. Tanizaki's son], the maid Yasuko and her sister and the sister's
adorable little son, Ken-chan; Akome; the parents of Akome's friend
Kaoru, who's now a student at UBC [University of British Columbia];
Ms. Uchida, of the Suntory Gallery, who helped last year with the
Yumeji painting for *Naomi*; and several people I didn't know.

Mrs. Tanizaki looked well and happy; Seiji was particularly friendly and kind and invited me to look him up in Osaka—he
knows some good eating places there. (He works in Osaka now, lives
in Yugawara, and has a room in Ashiya provided by his employer.)
Emiko, too, was very kind. The presents Mrs. Tanizaki opened while
I was there—a purse, *zōri*—were lavish; my ¥1600 rabbit doll is ab-
surd by comparison, but I expect she'll like it. Seiji admired my tie.
The restaurant still uses chairs of the same design as the one that
collapsed under me at my birthday party in 1980. We had some good
laughs recalling that. (My diary, 8/19/86)

Mrs. Tanizaki called. She sounds well but says she's having difficulty writing because of pain in her right hand. She said she'd call
tomorrow morning and asked what time I'd be getting up. "Probably
before you," I said, thinking of jet lag, since I'd just arrived from
California. She laughed, not thinking of jet lag, and said "You've got
me there!" (「いわれました、いわれました。」). (12/27/86)

A long, chatty call from Mrs. Tanizaki. A Tanizaki library (資料館) is due to open in Ashiya in July 1988; she wants to stay well enough to attend the opening and hopes that I can come. She plans to move to a "mansion" (condo) near Baji Park (馬事公苑), in Setagaya, in June. For New Year's she'll return to Yugawara, and hopes that I can visit after January 5. Other matters: She says living so long isn't necessarily a happy (うれしい) thing; she's never experienced jet lag and asked what it's like; her son has been asking about me and wants to introduce me to good food in Osaka. (12/28/86)

Our plan was that I'd arrive at the Kanzes' at a little past noon. Mrs. Tanizaki called this morning to ask me to be about thirty minutes late—12:30 or 1:00. While I was in the library [of International House], she called again and left a message that she'd arrive at I-House at 12:30. At 12:15 she called again to tell me she'd be here in about 30 minutes. This was all typical—her thoughtfulness, her tendency to be late, her tendency to shift schedules. She arrived at 12:45, and we chatted in the lobby for a few minutes. She gave me a Christian Dior tie (Dior is her favorite, she says, and she emphasized that this one was imported, not made in Japan.) It's grey-blue with a sort of herringbone pattern, dark blue diagonals, and pale blue circles. She also gave me the winter 1987 special issue of *Chūō Kōron*, containing part seven of her autobiography, the section on her mother. The response to her autobiography has been good, she said, but writing so much has caused nerve-related pain in her right arm. Tanizaki had the same problem, exacerbated by calcium deposits in his neck and shoulder. I asked if she couldn't dictate, as Tanizaki did. She said she writes a draft and has someone copy it out.

Twice during the day she said, rather emphatically, "longevity isn't fun" (長生きをするのは幸せではない). Though she's in pretty good shape for eighty-four, she says, she's always discovering pains in places she was never aware of before; new problems are always coming up; friends and associates disappear.

I asked her what she thinks about life after death. She spoke of accounts by people who had "died" (e.g., during surgery) and then "come back." Their reports are startlingly alike—of a beautiful, bright world full of blossoms, where all those who went before are present to meet again, and where all earthly problems, such as blindness, are cured. At the same time, she says she has trouble believing in a soul (霊魂) that survives after death; yet she has experienced things since Tanizaki's death that make her think it's possible—but that's a long story, she said, and she'll tell me another time.

Mrs. Tanizaki spoke of travel: friends have urged her to go at least to Hawaii—first class is so comfortable, and one can lie down. In his later years, Tanizaki had no interest in visiting Europe; he felt more affinity with China. (12/30/86)

MATSUKO: One of Mrs. Tanizaki's poems has been called one of the great waka of the Shōwa period [1926–89] (昭和の名歌):

昭和八年
京都高雄山の地蔵院に在りて春琴抄完成近き頃に贈る
夕霞　棚引く頃は　佐保姫の　姿をかりて　訪はましも
　のを

[1933
*Sent [to Tanizaki] when [he was] at Jizōin, on Mt. Takao, in Kyoto,
　and had nearly completed* A Portrait of Shunkin
*As the evening haze of spring drifts above, I wish I could borrow
　Saohime's form and visit you.*
『十八公子家集』, p. 2] (1/15/88)

Mrs. Tanizaki taught us Tanizaki's poem about her propensity to weep:

こゑあけて　怐性もなく　泣きたまふ　頑是なき人　わが
　　ともし妻

[*The artless one who wails aloud without restraint—my precious
　wife*

『谷崎潤一郎歌集』, p. 309, composed in 1956.] (1/15/88)

Mrs. Tanizaki said she wanted to deliver something to me the day
before I left. I called her after breakfast. She's fighting a cold and
so quickly accepted my offer to go to her rather than her coming
here. We decided on 4:00. Mrs. Tanizaki was attended by Emiko; the
servants had the day off. As usual, I was greeted at the front door.
(The only time I was shown inside was on the first visit, in 1971.)
They're embarrassed by the mess and the dogs. Mrs. Tanizaki was
beautifully dressed, though her hair looked slightly out of order.
After giving me a bag of three gifts for my mother and a couple of
paperbacks (including a copy of her second memoir), she put on a
coat (with Emiko's help) and insisted on seeing me as far as the end
of the driveway. I protested, but she was not to be deterred. There
was a chilly breeze, and the driveway is a moderately steep incline,
up from the street. Slowly, with Emiko, she walked down the drive
with me and watched and waved until I rounded the corner at the
end of the block. On January 15, too, when I escorted her home,
she and Emiko stood together—Emiko slightly behind her, looking
over her shoulder—as our taxi cautiously backed down the driveway.
Mrs. Tanizaki has been advised not to walk alone, for fear of falling.
She *is* careful. Yesterday, at the first word of Hideo's cold, she went
to her doctor for an antibiotic injection. She said she's worried about
pneumonia. She also gave me an ad for the new deluxe edition of
『細雪』 (*The Makioka Sisters*) and said she'd send me a copy. [This
was the next to last time I saw her.] (My diary, 1/17/88)

　　I met Emiko in Aoyama, near the hospital where Mrs. Tanizaki
was staying. Though Mrs. Tanizaki had been feeling better when

we arranged this meeting, Emiko told me now that her mother had declined since then, but wanted to see me anyway. Emiko showed me to the room. It was beautifully decorated—Mrs. Tanizaki always wanted to be surrounded by beauty. She lay on her side in bed as a nurse massaged her back. She looked tiny and weak. (My diary, 11/25/89)

TANIZAKI SHŪHEI

Born in 1908 (and so twenty-two years younger than Jun'ichirō); eighth child in the family; lives in Yokosuka and works for the publisher Heibonsha. He used a number of English words in his conversation, in the most natural way; though he didn't speak English to us [Paul McCarthy and me], I had the impression that he knows a good deal of English. At first he was rather reserved, but with wine (老酒) he loosened up and talked a good deal. Like Jun'ichirō, he has firm opinions (意見がはっきりしている) and is stubborn, if polite, in defending them. He was curious about American food and about our backgrounds (why we got interested in Japan). Whenever there was a lull in the conversation, he would fill it with a question. He has a striking physical resemblance to Jun'ichirō: short, stout, a bit clumsy, round head, balding, age spots on his forehead. Mrs. Tanizaki said that he didn't used to look like her husband, but has increasingly come to resemble him with age. He had consumption (he used the English word) and coughs a good deal. What works of his brother's does he like? *Some Prefer Nettles, Captain Shigemoto's Mother.* He doesn't care for the early works, but, for "family reasons," he made an exception for "Sorrows of a Heretic." He doesn't like "abnormal" works (again, he used English; he also used 変態). Very fussy about food, he said that he and his brother are very similar in that regard. Almost at the beginning of the meal he said:

"It doesn't taste good. I apologize." (おいしくありませんね。どうもすみません。)

"But I think it's delicious" (いいえ、おいしいとおもいますが), I said.

"No, no, it doesn't taste good" (いいえ、いいえ、おいしくありません).

Through the whole meal he hardly ate anything, though he drank a lot of wine. Everyone turned to him when there was a decision to be made on the menu.

Next to food, his favorite topic of conversation was language.

His voice is not so strong as his brother's, according to Mrs. Tanizaki; it's a bit thin; he talks fast, with that special courtesy and graciousness that Meiji people had.

He spent years growing up with Ayuko; she's only eight years younger than he, and so they're more like siblings than like uncle and niece. She calls him "Shū-chan."

His manner is gentle. According to Mrs. Tanizaki, there was a sternness (きびしさ) in her husband, which Shūhei lacks.

When I asked him about his children, he said he has three girls and a boy. The boy is thirty-two, though he had trouble remembering his age and had to ask Ayuko. He said in so many words, "I don't care for boys" (男の子は好きじゃない), though he wasn't speaking specifically of his son.

I was struck by the contrast between Mrs. Tanizaki, on the one hand, and Shūhei and Ayuko on the other. The latter two are jolly, portly, and earthier than Mrs. Tanizaki; Mrs. Tanizaki seems aristocratic, fragile, sublime by comparison. No doubt the contrast appealed to Tanizaki.

The 1923 earthquake, as described by Shūhei: It began with a frightening groan from the earth. Then the ground swelled and rolled; it didn't just move side-to-side.

Shūhei lamented the rapidity of change in Japan and said that the pace is accelerating. His own toys, games, and activities as a child were the same as those described in Tanizaki's *Childhood Years* (幼少時代, 1955), despite the twenty-two-year difference in their ages. Times changed more slowly in Meiji Japan, he said.

Tanizaki thought of sending Shūhei to Gyōsei Elementary School (暁星, École de l'Étoile du Matin, in Tokyo), so that Shūhei could accompany him to France as his interpreter.

In around 1930, Shūhei went to Tokyo (from Tanizaki's home in Western Japan, where he had been living since his parents' death) to go to school; after that time, he met his brother occasionally but didn't have much contact with him. (7/12/77)

Takeda Ayuko said that her father intended to go to Europe before the 1923 earthquake. Shūhei wondered what course Tanizaki's career and writing might have taken had he gone to Europe as planned: he sounded as though he regretted that Tanizaki hadn't gone. Mrs. Tanizaki said that her husband wanted to take Shigeko, who had studied French, to France after he finished his first *Genji* translation, but the war interfered. (7/12/77)

Mrs. Tanizaki said that Maruya Saiichi praised Shūhei's Tokyo speech as pure and beautiful. (1/15/88)

After treating us to an eel lunch in Kōjimachi, Shūhei took me and a younger writer, who looked up to him as her mentor, to Kōrakuen. As we strolled through the garden, Shūhei quizzed her on the names of trees and shrubs. She failed the test. "I'm astonished" (あきれましたね), he said. A writer needs to know these things. (Summer 1985)

TAKEDA AYUKO

My impressions of Ayuko: Very friendly from the first. Round face, jolly—she smiles and laughs a lot. She closely resembles her father and looks younger than her sixty-one years. (I didn't have much opportunity to talk with her; I was seated next to Shūhei, but across the table from Ayuko.)

Ayuko's name: Tanizaki's friend Kishi Iwao suggested several fish names for him [to consider]; Tanizaki picked "ayu" ("trout") from among them. Sometimes in his letters to her he wrote her name 安遊.

Ayuko remembers going to Mt. Kōya with her parents [in 1922]. They ascended the mountain in sedan chairs (籠). The path was lined with lepers, begging: people would be prepared with small change and hand a coin to each one. The family went to the Okunoin at night, where they saw a woman suffering an epileptic fit. It was terrifying. (7/12/77)

Fig. 1. Anthony Chambers with Loyal Dog
Hachikō and Edward Seidensticker, in
Shibuya, September 1977

Fig. 2. Paul McCarthy, Tanizaki Matsuko, and
Anthony Chambers at Mrs. Tanizaki's house in
Yugawara, July 4, 1977

Fig. 3. Anthony Chambers with Tanizaki Matsuko. "After dinner we moved to the spacious and relaxing lobby and asked a hotel man to take several photos of us. She was in no hurry; she was glad to be away from the telephone" (August 17, 1985).

Fig. 4. Anthony Chambers with Tanizaki Matsuko. "She looked tired at first, but seemed to get livelier as the evening went on" (August 13, 1986).

Fig. 5. Anthony Chambers with
Tanizaki Shūhei after lunch in
Kōjimachi. "He talks fast, with
that special courtesy and gra-
ciousness that Meiji people had"
(Summer 1985).

Fig. 6. Anthony Chambers, Kanze
Emiko, Tanizaki Matsuko, and
Watanabe Seiji at Mrs. Tanizaki's
seventy-seventh birthday dinner,
August 1980.

Fig. 7. Tanizaki Matsuko and Anthony Chambers at
Mrs. Tanizaki's eighty-third birthday party. "Mrs.
Tanizaki looked well and happy" (August 1986).

Fig. 8. Anthony Chambers with Mrs. Tanizaki and her fan club. "The gathering of women before him was like a flower garden seen for the first time, sparkling with color and redolent of strange incense" (July 3, 1985).

Fig. 9. Robert Campbell (*far left*), Kanze Akome (*third from left*), Kanze Emiko (*third from right*), and Tanizaki Matsuko (*far right*) at Anthony Chambers's thirty-seventh birthday party. "Everything seems to be falling tonight," Mrs. Tanizaki said (July 1, 1980).

◾ REFERENCES ◾

Bernardi, Joanne. *Writing in Light: The Silent Scenario and the Japanese Pure Film Movement*. Wayne State University Press, 2001.

Bienati, Luisa, and Bonaventura Ruperti, eds. *The Grand Old Man and the Great Tradition: Essays on Tanizaki Jun'ichirō in Honor of Adriana Boscaro*. University of Michigan Press, 2009.

Boscaro, Adriana. *Tanizaki in Western Languages: A Bibliography of Translations and Studies*. University of Michigan Press, 1999.

Boscaro, Adriana, and Anthony Chambers, eds. *A Tanizaki Feast: The International Symposium in Venice*. University of Michigan Press, 1994.

Chambers, Anthony H. *The Secret Window: Ideal Worlds in Tanizaki's Fiction*. Harvard University Asia Center, 1994.

Gessel, Van C. *Three Modern Novelists*. Kodansha International, 1994.

Ito, Ken. *Visions of Desire: Tanizaki's Fictional Worlds*. Stanford University Press, 1991.

Keene, Donald. *Dawn to the West*. Vol. 1: *Fiction*. Holt, Rinehart and Winston, 1984.

Long, Margherita. *This Perversion Called Love: Reading Tanizaki, Feminist Theory, and Freud*. Stanford University Press, 2009.

Maruya Saiichi. *Singular Rebellion*. Translated by Dennis Keene. Kodansha America, 1986.

Murasaki Shikibu. *The Tale of Genji*. Translated by Royall Tyler. Viking, 2001.

野口尚吾、『伝記谷崎潤一郎』, 1972, 改訂新版, 1974. Biography of Tanizaki Jun'ichirō by Nomura Shōgo.

Seidensticker, Edward. "Tanizaki Jun-ichirō, 1886–1965." *Monumenta Nipponica* 21:3–4 (1966): 249–65.

谷崎 潤一郎 (著), 千葉 俊二 (編集). 『谷崎潤一郎の恋文—松子・重子姉妹との書簡集』, 中央公論新社, 2015. Love letters of Tanizaki Jun'ichirō, Tanizaki Matsuko, and her sister Watanabe Shigeko.

谷崎潤一郎.『谷崎潤一郎歌集』. 湯川書房, 1977. Tanizaki Jun'ichirō's collected poems.

谷崎潤一郎.『谷崎潤一郎全集』, 28 vols. 中央公論社, 1966–68. Complete works of Tanizaki Jun'ichirō. A more comprehensive "complete works," in 26 volumes, was published 2015-17 by 中央公論新社.

谷崎松子.『倚松庵の夢』. 中央公論社, 1967. Tanizaki Matsuko's first memoir.

谷崎松子. 『湘竹居の思い出』. 中央公論社, 1983. Tanizaki Matsuko's second memoir.

谷崎松子. 『蘆辺の夢』. 中央公論社, 1998. Tanizaki Matsuko's third memoir, with essays, published posthumously.

谷崎松子.『十八公子家集』. 五月書房, 1979. Tanizaki Matsuko's collected poetry.

谷崎終平.『懐かしき人々・兄潤一郎とその周辺』. 文藝春秋, 1989. Tanizaki Shūhei's memoir.

Tawara Machi. *Salad Anniversary*. Translated by Juliet Winters Carpenter. Kodansha America, 1990.

Uno Chiyo. *The Old Woman, the Wife, and the Archer: Three Modern Japanese Short Novels*. Translated by Donald Keene. Constable, 1962. Includes *Ohan*.

A Cat, a Man, and Two Women. Translated by Paul McCarthy. Kodansha International, 1990. Reissued by New Directions, 2016. Includes "The Little Kingdom."

Childhood Years: A Memoir. Translated by Paul McCarthy. Kodansha International, 1988. Reissued by the University of Michigan Press, 2017.

Devils in Daylight. Translated by J. Keith Vincent. New Directions, 2017.

Diary of a Mad Old Man. Translated by Howard Hibbett. Knopf, 1965.

The Gourmet Club: A Sextet. Translated by Anthony H. Chambers and Paul McCarthy. Kodansha International, 2001. Reissued by the University of Michigan Press, 2017.

In Black and White. Translated by Phillis I. Lyons. Columbia University Press, forthcoming in 2017.

In Praise of Shadows. Translated by Thomas J. Harper and Edward G. Seidensticker. Leete's Island Books, 1977.

The Key. Translated by Howard Hibbett. Knopf, 1961.

The Maids. Translated by Michael P. Cronin. New Directions, 2017.

The Makioka Sisters. Translated by Edward Seidensticker. Knopf, 1957.

Naomi. Translated by Anthony H. Chambers. Knopf, 1985.

Quicksand. Translated by Howard Hibbett. Knopf, 1994.

Red Roofs and Other Stories. Translated by Anthony H. Chambers and Paul McCarthy. University of Michigan Press, 2016.

The Reed Cutter and Captain Shigemoto's Mother: Two Novellas. Translated by Anthony H. Chambers. Knopf, 1994.

The Secret History of the Lord of Musashi and Arrowroot: Two Novellas. Translated by Anthony H. Chambers. Knopf, 1982.

Seven Japanese Tales. Translated by Howard Hibbett. Knopf, 1963.

Some Prefer Nettles. Translated by Edward Seidensticker. Knopf, 1955.